REGIONAL ITALIAN COOKING

By Valentina Harris
Illustrated by David Sim

SAINSBURY · WALKER BOOKS

Per le donne Italiane della mia vita
Katia, Leo, Benedetta
e la mia meravigliosa mamma Fiammetta

SAINSBURY CLASSIC COOKBOOKS

Series editor: Jill Norman
Designer: Jim Bunker

Published exclusively for
J Sainsbury plc
Stamford Street London SE1 9LL
by Walker Books Ltd
184-192 Drummond Street
London NW1 3HP

First published 1986

ISBN 0-7445-0652-2

CONTENTS

INTRODUCTION 9

SOUPS & STARTERS 10

TRENTINO-ALTO ADIGE 18

FRIULI-VENEZIA GIULIA 19

VENETO 20

PASTA, GNOCCHI AND RISOTTO 22

LOMBARDY 32

PIEDMONT 33

LIGURIA 34

PIZZA, EGG AND CHEESE DISHES 36

EMILIA-ROMAGNA 44

TUSCANY 45

FISH DISHES 46

UMBRIA 52

LE MARCHE 53

MEAT DISHES 54

LAZIO 60

ABRUZZO-MOLISE 61

POULTRY & GAME DISHES 62

CAMPANIA 68

BASILICATA-LUCANIA 69

VEGETABLE DISHES 70

APULIA 78

CALABRIA 79

CAKES AND DESSERTS 80

SICILY 88

SARDINIA 89

GLOSSARY 91

INDEX 93

INTRODUCTION

Italy is a land of contrasts, of snowy mountains, sandy beaches, historic monuments and soft green hills. Anybody who comes to Italy will return again and again – whether they throw coins in the fountain or not. Yet how is it that the Austrian-flavoured air of the high Friuli mountains can be under the same flag as sun-baked Sicily or rugged, poverty-stricken Basilicata? Surely this is what makes it the fascinating country it is, with many faces to inspire and attract the visitor.

The food of each region is an almost perfect mirror reflection of its climate, geography, character and economy. Though in some cases the differences are subtle, thanks to modern intercommunication and blending of boundaries, it only takes a little careful searching to find the essence of each region's cuisine; the techniques, flavours and ingredients that make the food of Apulia really her own; the traditions that seal an inimitable Tuscan speciality.

In this book I have tried to give the reader a balanced mix of regional dishes, choosing some of the more unusual and original as well as some of the better known. I have also tried to give an idea of Italy as a country that has very distinct regions; this beautiful peninsula has only been united since 1841 and there are times when you really feel that the people are still getting used to the idea of belonging to one nation!

In the far northern regions like the Alto Adige, you will find the food Germanic – lots of sauerkraut, sausages and horseradish. Move west and you will come to Piedmont with all its delicious creamy, truffle-speckled dishes that remind you constantly that this was once a province of France. Come down south to Naples and its surrounding area and the bright colours and vivid flavours immediately bring the typical Spanish kitchen to mind. The influence of all its previous rulers is felt throughout the country's culture, history and art – so why not in the kitchen?

Italian gastronomy is steeped in history and tradition, and has always rightfully held its place as one of the world's leading gourmet havens. Yet this is a cuisine that belongs to the people, it cannot boast of famous chefs who concoct sophisticated and elaborate dishes. The Italians have simply taken their best local ingredients, added imagination, flair and common sense, a pinch of tradition and a sprinkle of history to emerge finally with a marvellous variety of delectable local specialities which have become famous the world over and are hard to beat for balance and flavour. A recent survey suggested that southern Italian cuisine is the healthiest in the world – careful examination will tell you why. The southern regions have so little to cook with, there is almost no red meat, plenty of fish, masses of fruit and vegetables, no butter as such and excellent wine and olive oil.

These recipes are mostly personal favourites which I believe give a true picture of each region's own cooking. For anybody who has been to Italy and sampled the delights of the food, here is your chance to re-create the wonders of your stay in your own kitchen. What better way to brighten a snowy English February than with a steaming plate of real minestrone or creamy risotto? What better way to complement our fresh green summers than by preparing marvellously coloured dishes of peppers and aubergines like Cianfotta from Campania or Piatto d'erbe alla Lucana? What friendlier way to set off your dinner parties than by beginning with a superb Bagna Cauda? So here it is, a collection of recipes and information about Italy, my Italy. All that remains for me to say is ... Buon Appetito.

Valentina Harris

1
SOUPS & STARTERS

FENNEL SOUP

ZUPPA DI FINOCCHI

CALABRIA

SERVES 6-8

5 large fennel bulbs	4 tablespoons olive oil
1 clove garlic, chopped	salt
fistful of parsley, chopped	6 small slices of toasted bread

Remove coarse outer section from fennel, then slice the rest of each vegetable finely. Place in a large saucepan with the garlic and parsley and fry gently in the oil.

Add 2 pt/1.2 litres cold water and season with salt. Stir and bring to the boil. As soon as the soup boils, reduce the heat and simmer gently until the fennel is falling apart, about 40 minutes.

Place the toast in the bottom of the soup tureen, pour the soup over it and serve. No cheese is required with this soup.

BAKED SEAFOOD ON TOAST

CROSTINI DI MARE ALLA GENOVESE

LIGURIA

SERVES 4

a large loaf of white or brown bread	3 tablespoons butter
2 lb/1 kg assorted seafood (mussels, oysters, clams, and any others available)	2 tablespoons fresh breadcrumbs
	salt
	3 tablespoons olive oil
2 tablespoons chopped parsley	pinch of chilli pepper

Slice the bread into fairly thick slices, then scoop a little of the soft centre out of each slice to form a little dip in each one. Toast each slice on both sides.

Clean all the seafood and cook it briefly to open the shells (see p. 27). Remove the shells. Arrange all the seafood on the slices of toasted bread, filling in the dip. Sprinkle with the chilli.

10

Fry together the parsley, butter and breadcrumbs and coat the seafood with the mixture. Sprinkle with salt and dribble olive oil over the top. Bake in a medium-hot oven gas 4/350°F/180°C for 10 minutes.
Serve hot as an antipasto (starter).

HOT GARLIC AND ANCHOVY DIP

BAGNA CAUDA

PIEDMONT

SERVES 4-6

4 oz/125 g canned salted anchovies, boned and washed, or equivalent anchovy paste

2 oz/50 g unsalted butter

6 large cloves garlic, finely sliced

½ pt/300 ml olive oil

For this dish you will need a fondue set; in Piedmont it would traditionally be made of terracotta.

The bagna can be prepared on a very low heat on the cooker as soon as everyone is ready to eat – it will take about 15 minutes to prepare.

Chop up the anchovies and mash them a little to form a smooth cream. Melt the butter in the fondue pot over the very lowest heat and add the garlic cloves to it. Let them soften, then add the anchovies and mix together. Finally add the oil and allow to simmer very gently for 10 minutes before bringing to the table and setting on top of your fondue flame. The result should be a hot, thickish sauce. But hot is really the operative word.

Into this sauce it is traditional to dip raw vegetables sliced into strips, or sometimes raw meat which has been marinated in water and lemon juice, or cooked peperoni. The vegetables used are usually crunchy cabbage leaves, tender cauliflower florets, Jerusalem artichokes and sweet red, yellow or green peppers.

VARIATIONS

Different parts of the region have other versions of the bagna. For example, in the Valle del Belbo, the garlic is allowed to soak for several hours in milk before being used, and then it is cooked for a very long time – all this is to render it more digestible. In other parts, they add walnuts to the mixture, chopped very finely to give just a flavour. In Monferrato they add a half glass of Barbera to the other ingredients, and in the Albese the garlic is pounded and a little bagna is always left in the pot, so that everyone can scramble some eggs in the bottom.

PEPPERS AND ANCHOVIES WITH GARLIC

ANTIPASTO DI PEPERONI

PIEDMONT

SERVES 4-6

3½ oz/100 g canned or salted anchovies

2 large cloves garlic

3 tablespoons olive oil

1 oz/25 g butter

3 tablespoons milk

4 yellow peppers, thick and fleshy

Remove the bones from the anchovies and wash them carefully to remove salt and oil. Chop very finely with the garlic. Fry the garlic and anchovy mixture in the olive oil and butter over low heat, stirring constantly.

Cut the peppers in half, remove the white stringy bits and the seeds, then cut into smallish pieces. Add the milk to the frying mixture and stir carefully to make it creamy. Add the peppers and stir together.

Cook for about 15 minutes or until the peppers are just soft. Turn the anchovy mixture over the peppers often so that they absorb as much flavour as possible.

Serve as a hot antipasto with crusty bread.

GOOD FRIDAY SOUP

ZUPPA DEL VENERDI SANTO

LAZIO

SERVES 6-8

1 salted anchovy, bones removed, washed and chopped, or 2 canned anchovies, or 1 teaspoon anchovy paste

1 large clove garlic, crushed

4 tablespoons chopped parsley

4 tablespoons passata* diluted in a ladleful of warm fish stock

6 tablespoons olive oil

2 pt/1.2 litres fish stock

5 oz/150 g scampi tails, boiled, peeled and cut into strips

10 oz/300 g lobster meat, boiled and sliced into thin strips

pinch of chilli pepper

4 oz/125 g croûtons, kept warm

Fry the anchovy, garlic and parsley in the olive oil, mixing all the time. When well blended together, add the passata diluted with the fish stock and stir thoroughly. Add the rest of the fish stock and simmer gently for about 30 minutes. Put in the scampi tails, lobster and chilli pepper. Heat through and then pour into a soup tureen, sprinkle the croûtons on top and serve at once.

---

*For more detailed information about terms marked with an asterisk, see glossary p. 91.

BROAD BEAN SOUP

FAVATA

SARDINIA

SERVES 6-8

10 oz/300 g sausages, chopped (coarse chipolatas would be best)

13 oz/400 g belly of pork, diced

10 oz/300 g streaky bacon, chopped

1 large onion, chopped

1 large carrot, chopped

1 large stick celery, chopped

2 large tomatoes, peeled and chopped, seeds discarded

13 oz/400 g broad beans

1 small savoy cabbage, shredded

pinch of dill

1 clove garlic, crushed

salt and pepper

Place the sausages, belly of pork and bacon on the bottom of the soup pot, with the onion, carrot and celery. Fry together in the fat from the meat until just beginning to soften, then add the tomatoes and mix together.

Put in the broad beans and cover with 5 pt/ 3 litres cold water, mix thoroughly, cover with a lid and simmer gently for about 1½ hours. Then add the cabbage, dill, garlic, salt and pepper. Mix thoroughly and continue to simmer for a further 1½ hours. Serve with hunks of bread.

13

FISH SOUP

CIUPPIN

LIGURIA

SERVES 6-8

3 lb/1.5 kg assorted fresh fish (go for whatever is in season and freshly available, the success of the dish depends upon the wide variety of fish included)

1 onion, chopped finely

1 stick celery, chopped finely

fistful of parsley, chopped finely

1 clove garlic, chopped finely

1 carrot, chopped finely

4 tablespoons olive oil

1 glass dry white wine

3 large ripe tomatoes or one 8 oz/250 g can tomatoes

2½ pt/1.5 litres boiling water

salt and pepper

1 large slice coarse bread per person, fried in olive oil or toasted in the oven

Clean and wash all the fish, leaving the larger scales on them, and set aside.

Fry the onion, carrot, celery, parsley and garlic in the olive oil. When the onion is transparent, add the wine. Boil fiercely for a few minutes to evaporate the fumes from the wine, then add the tomatoes – if using fresh ones, peel, chop and discard all seeds.

Add the boiling water, season and stir. Place a lid on the pot and simmer for 20 minutes. Then put in the fish, beginning with the kinds that will take the longest to cook and working your way through to the ones that cook quickly.

When all the fish is cooked through very thoroughly, sieve it all into another saucepan. Add a little boiling water if required. What you should end up with is a smooth velvety soup. Taste and adjust seasoning as required. Bring back to the boil and serve with fried or toasted bread.

MILANESE MINESTRONE

MINESTRONE ALLA MILANESE

LOMBARDY

SERVES 6-8

2 cloves garlic

2 oz/50 g lard

fistful of parsley, chopped

1 large onion, chopped

3 oz/75 g streaky smoked bacon, chopped

1 strip belly of pork, chopped into squares

2 courgettes, sliced

2 large carrots, sliced

2 sticks celery, chopped

1 lb/500 g fresh tomatoes, peeled, deseeded and chopped

3 large floury potatoes, peeled and left whole

8 basil leaves

2 sage leaves

8 oz/250 g borlotti beans (canned or fresh)

salt and pepper

1 lb/500 g peas

½ small savoy cabbage, chopped coarsely

7 oz/200 g Easy Cook Italian rice or small pasta*

8 tablespoons Parmesan,* grated

There are so many different variations of this popular dish, that I have given the one which is considered to be the most widely appreciated. Of course, although minestrone is originally a Milanese dish, there are versions of it to be found in other parts of Italy as well. In Milan the differences of opinion are all concerned with the use of the bacon – some sprinkle it over the finished soup, some fry it with the lard, some people don't use it at all!

Chop the garlic, lard and parsley together into a smooth paste. Melt the lard, and fry the onion, bacon, belly of pork, garlic and parsley paste together in the bottom of a very large pot. Stir it to prevent sticking or overbrowning, and when the onion is soft put in the courgettes, carrots, celery, potatoes, tomatoes, basil and sage leaves.

Stir thoroughly, pour in 5 pt/3 litres water, stir again, then add the borlotti beans. Season and bring to the boil. Place a lid on the pot and simmer slowly for about 3 hours.

Then put in the peas, and cook for a further 30 minutes. Finally, add the chopped cabbage and the rice. The minestrone is ready when the rice is soft. If the potatoes have not fallen apart in the cooking, mash them with a fork.

Allow the minestrone to sit for about 20 minutes, off the heat, before serving. Ladle out into soup plates and sprinkle with Parmesan.

LENTIL AND BORAGE SOUP

MINESTRA DI LENTICCHIE E BORAGGINE

CAMPANIA

SERVES 6-8

4 oz/125 g brown lentils, soaked overnight in cold water	2 fistfuls of fresh borage, washed and chopped
7 oz/200 g ripe tomatoes, peeled and chopped, seeds discarded	3 tablespoons olive oil
	salt and pepper
	4 slices coarse bread

When the lentils have soaked, scoop off all those which have come to the surface and throw them away. Pour the rest into a colander and wash them in cold water.

Place them in a saucepan, cover with 2½ pt/1.5 litres cold water, and bring to the boil. Turn down the heat and simmer gently until almost cooked, then add the borage, tomatoes, oil, and a little salt and pepper to taste. Continue to cook the soup for a further 30 minutes over gentle heat, stirring occasionally.

Lay the slices of bread in the bottom of a soup tureen, pour the soup over the bread and serve.

FLORENTINE BEAN SOUP

ZUPPA DI FAGIOLI ALLA FIORENTINA

TUSCANY

SERVES 6-8

2 onions, chopped coarsely	10 oz/300 g dark outer leaves of a savoy cabbage, washed and cut into largish pieces
1 clove garlic, chopped	
8 tablespoons virgin olive oil	
1 carrot, chopped	salt and pepper
1 leek, chopped	a sprig of rosemary
1 extra large ripe tomato, chopped	a sprig of thyme
	2 cloves garlic, slightly crushed
2 lb/1 kg dried borlotti beans, soaked overnight in cold water, drained and washed	4 slices brown bread toasted, then rubbed with a garlic clove
1 ham bone	6 tablespoons Parmesan,* grated

Fry the onions and garlic in half the oil until transparent, then add the carrot, leek and tomato. Mix together and cook until softened, then add the beans, ham bone and 2½ pt/1.5 litres cold water. Season with a little salt and simmer gently until the beans are cooked – about 1½ hours.

When the beans are soft, remove the bone and a ladleful of beans. Put the ladleful of whole beans to one side and throw the bone away. Sieve everything else in the pot. Put the soup back on a low heat, adding beans and cabbage leaves, season and stir.

In a little saucepan, heat the remaining olive oil with the rosemary, thyme and garlic. Heat gently and, after about 10 minutes, stir it into the soup.

Place the garlic toast in the bottom of a soup tureen, pour the soup over it and sprinkle with the Parmesan before serving.

VARIATION

The leftovers of this soup are used to make another traditional Florentine speciality called Ribollita. Pour the leftover soup into an ovenproof dish and completely cover it with sliced onions. Then bake it in a hot oven until the onion has formed a crisp golden crust.

CHICKEN SOUP

ZUPPA DI POLLO

PIEDMONT

SERVES 6-8

10 oz/300 g cooked chicken, white meat only, minced	2 pt/1.2 litres best chicken stock
pinch of nutmeg	3 sticks celery, chopped coarsely
4 oz/125 g Parmesan,* grated	croûtons or toasted brown bread
salt and pepper	

Mix the chicken with the nutmeg, Parmesan, salt and pepper in a small bowl. Bring the stock to the boil with the celery in it, and then simmer until the celery has softened.

Remove celery, process to a smooth purée and return to the soup. Add in the chicken mixture and simmer for a further 5 minutes. Serve at once with croûtons or toasted brown bread.

TRENTINO-ALTO ADIGE

The two zones which form this region were finally united in 1918, but there are great distinctions between them.

Trentino, named after the principal city of Trento, occupies the central part of the Adige valley and lies to the south of Alto Adige which was part of Austria until 1918 when it was renamed Venezia Tridentina. It was finally given its present name in 1948 yet the Austrians still refer to it as Süd Tirol. It is Italy's northernmost region, bordering on Switzerland, Austria, the Veneto and Lombardy; its southern tip touches the top end of the lovely lake Garda. The entire region is dominated by the Dolomites, the Alps and the Adamello mountain range. The principal cities are Bolzano to the north and Trento to the south.

The tourists in these parts can well be forgiven for thinking they have already crossed the border out of Italy as more than half the population in the north of the region speak German as a first language. There are German road signs, shop signs, TV shows, newspapers and schools alongside those in Italian. To confuse you even further, the inhabitants of the Dolomites speak Ladino, a language derived from Latin but totally different from Italian. Today tourism is the region's principal source of commerce and it is well organised with typical Germanic efficiency.

The food is heavily influenced by the region's Austrian and Swiss neighbours. Many dishes are traditional Tirolese specialities although some have been given a more Mediterranean feel. You'll find plenty of strudel and würstel here but also excellent ravioli and gnocchi, although they may be called knödel and türtlen!

The region is also renowned for its marvellous lean stuffed roasts and freshwater fish. A traditional speciality is smoked meat – all different kinds of meat from pork to poultry, horse meat and beef. They are smoked very slowly for a long time, then served with brown bread and butter and pickles, or boiled until soft and crumbling and served with steaming dishes of sauerkraut. Cabbages grow in endless neat rows in all the fields and these, soaked in vinegar and water to become sauerkraut, are almost the only vegetable eaten in these mountains apart from potatoes. Sauerkraut is perfect for serving with all the fatty pork which is consumed in abundance. The potatoes are boiled and sliced, then served with vinegar and black pepper. It is one of the very few places in Italy where pasta will be served as an accompaniment to the main course.

Everything about the food of this region reflects the cold climate; even in summer the temperature remains fairly cool and in winter the snow never seems to stop. Food here is rich and hearty with wonderfully colourful pastries and cakes to brighten up the table, usually smothered with delicious whipped cream. Look out for superb fritters filled with fruit or jam, omelettes oozing hot bubbling fruit preserves, incredibly rich hot chocolate, thick and gooey under a mountain of white, sweet whipped cream.

The local specialities are just the kind of thing you want after a day skiing or walking out in the cold and to wash it all down you'll discover marvellous local beer as well as an enormous variety of wines. The best known are the Pinot Bianco with its yellow colouring with greenish tints and delicious flavour that makes a perfect aperitif when served chilled, and the dark red Pinot Nero which is equally delicious. Worth a try with special meals is the subtle Lagrein, a ruby to garnet coloured sparkling wine with a lovely soft flavour. The unmistakable Merlot Trentino has a harmonious flavour and a colour that goes from ruby red to pink. Finally, to serve with any strong flavoured fish I would recommend Traminer, with its soft, generous, fruity flavour and deep straw yellow colouring.

FRIULI-VENEZIA GIULIA

The easternmost region of Italy, bounded by rivers and the Julian and Carnic Alps, it borders with Austria to the north and with Yugoslavia to the east. It is a land of simplicity and of people who enjoy eating with gusto and good humour.

Polenta reigns supreme, much more so than in neighbouring Veneto; it is served with imagination and flair: covered with cheese or meat; toasted and then smothered with thick slices of salame. Prosciutto di San Daniele comes from this region; it is the product of small fat pigs that are left to graze in quiet green valleys. Great care is taken in the selection and raising of cattle, and lamb and mutton are also excellent. Meat is preferred cooked on the spit over open fires so that an unmistakably herby smell fills the air.

The further you go towards Trieste, the more you feel the influence of Austrian and Yugoslavian cuisine. Here we find goulash served with foaming beer, boiled pork served with horseradish and Austrian sausages with mustard. Pizza is called pinza in these parts and bears little resemblance to its Neapolitan cousin. The most important part of any meal is the soup, which will be enough to keep anyone going for half a day! It is an immensely rich, thick concoction with meat, vegetables and often barley or coarse ground flour to make the whole thing even more substantial.

I cannot say that there is anything remotely subtle about the cuisine of Friuli-Venezia Giulia; the food is designed to fill you up and nourish you as much as possible. Even the desserts tend to be thick and heavy, using a great deal of dried fruit and nuts to fill pastry cases and cakes. Chestnuts are boiled or roasted and eaten with a glass of wine to finish off a meal.

The foothills of the region supply a great quantity of diverse wines, many of which are very dry with a trace of flint about them. Look out for the delicious Bianco del Collio which is a wine with a very short life that has to be drunk within the year. Marvellous to serve with desserts is the sweet refreshing Verduzzo which owes its distinctive flavour to the addition of raisins. Refosco Nostrano typifies the red wines of the region. It has a slightly sharp, flinty taste and is very refreshing. Pinot Grigio is perhaps the region's most famous wine. It varies in colour from greyish pink to straw yellow and has a very clean, sharp flavour that makes it perfect for serving with all kinds of fish.

19

VENETO

Situated in the north-eastern part of the Po valley this region is defined by the rivers which flow all around it: the Mincio, the Tagliamento, the Livenza, the Po, and the Garda. It is a region of enormously varied landscape with a vast mountainous area to the north which gives way to small hills which then turn into the lowlands where the rice grows. The lowlands stretch down to the sea and are criss-crossed by rivers and canals. It is an area of land which has been torn out of the water and drained, which becomes more like water dotted with islands as you get nearer to the coast.

The region is important for its agricultural production. Enormous quantities of vegetables and fruit are produced and high grade cattle thrive on the pasturelands of the flat plains which are interspersed with huge industrial complexes and busy roads. As always, when the land is fertile, the vine thrives and this region gives us such well known and excellent wines as Soave, Valpolicella and Bardolino.

Its principal city is, of course, the romantic and

beautiful Venice, but there are many other fabulous cities to visit in the region, and lovely little towns perched on hillsides, like Asolo in the province of Treviso. Out in the countryside between Venice, Padua and Treviso you will be able to see the splendid villas built by Venetian noblemen in order to have somewhere cool and unsmelly to spend the summer. They are a wonderful feast of architectural good taste and the enormous salons and gardens were the scenes for banquets and parties that have gone down in history.

Venetian cooking is fairly homely and straightforward. Simple dishes predominate and the onion is in evidence, as are all types of vegetables, beans, rice and spicy sauces. Very popular is the yellow polenta – corn meal boiled in water like porridge, then turned out onto a board, cooled and sliced before being served with stews, or cheese, or milk, or sometimes even fish.

The trademark of Venetian cookery is risotto, and of all of these the most famous must be the wonderful Risi e Bisi, a combination of rice and fresh peas cooked with good stock. Risotto in this region is never plain and smooth as in Lombardy; here it is always supplemented with meat, game, fish, seafood or vegetables of a thousand varieties. Considered always to be exclusively a first course, risotto from this area is rich enough to be a complete meal.

Pasta does not come into the picture very much, in fact they have even managed to grow a kind of rice with enormous grains which is a perfect substitute for pasta – but having said that, one must not forget the other emblem of the Venetian kitchen, the universal Pasta e Fagioli, a wondrous, thick, hearty bean and pasta soup.

Here and there you will discover recipes which have a hint of Byzantine or Oriental cuisine about them, dishes to which a handful of raisins and a generous touch of spices have been added and which makes them unlike any other Italian dish. There is a feel of ancient traditions about the cookery of this region, a feeling that people here have always really enjoyed a good meal and have relished its pleasures.

Stockfish (baccala) is widely used throughout the region, but also fresh fish and shellfish in great variety.

Lots of bright, vivacious wines accompany their simple fare. Superb Bianco di Conegliano has a sharp flinty flavour and a golden colour. Gambellara is a wine to serve with special meals; it is a dry, light, refreshing white wine. Cabernet di Treviso and Cabernet Franc are two delicious red wines with plenty of body. One of the most famous of the local wines is Prosecco, which comes in both still and sparkling forms and has a flavour which varies from sweet to fruity. The sparkling variety produces a great deal of foam. And of course, the aforementioned Soave, Valpolicella and Bardolino are famous the world over for their consistently fine quality.

2
PASTA, GNOCCHI AND RISOTTO

TAGLIATELLE WITH WALNUT AND GARLIC SAUCE

AGLIATA

PIEDMONT

SERVES 4

8 oz/250 g shelled
walnuts

3 oz/75 g soft white
breadcrumbs

¼ pt/150 ml milk (or
more as required)

3 cloves garlic, peeled and
cut into quarters

salt and pepper

13 oz/400 g dried
tagliatelle

3 oz/75 g unsalted butter

Soak the breadcrumbs in the milk – depending on
the type of bread used you may need more milk to
soak it well. Place all the pieces of walnut in the food
processor and process briefly. Add the garlic and
blend the mixture of garlic and walnuts to a smooth
purée – but it must remain crunchy with small pieces
of walnut left in.

Remove from the food processor and mix in the
milk and bread, without squeezing any milk out of
the bread. Season, stir and set aside to rest.

After about 30 minutes, bring a large pot of water
to the boil with a few pinches of salt. When the
water is at a rolling boil, toss in the tagliatelle, stir to
avoid sticking, and replace lid until the water has
returned to the boil. Remove lid and boil for the
required time (about 3-4 minutes).

Drain and transfer to a warm bowl, add the butter and toss, then pour over the garlic and walnut
sauce, toss again and bring to the table.

As the sauce is fairly unusual, it is sometimes
served separately in a sauce boat so that each person
can add as much as they wish to their pasta.

Traditionally this dish is served in the autumn,
when the new wine barrels are tapped and decanted
into bottles. No Parmesan cheese is normally served
with this dish.

PUMPKIN TORTELLI

TORTELLI DI ZUCCA

LOMBARDY

SERVES 8

5 lb/2.5 kg yellow pumpkin (with seeds and skin)

7 oz/200 g amaretti or ratafia biscuits, crushed to a powder

10 oz/300 g Italian pickled fruit (mostarda di frutta) or spicy apple chutney

10 oz/300 g Parmesan, * grated

large pinch of nutmeg

salt and pepper

juice of ½ lemon, strained

1½ lb/700 g strong white flour

6 eggs

8 oz/250 g butter, melted and kept warm

It is preferable to make the filling for the tortelli a day in advance, as it does improve the flavour enormously. The most important element of the recipe is the quality of the pumpkin. It must be firm and juicy with a good yellow colour. Cut it into pieces and remove the seeds, but leave on the rind. The pieces should be even-sized, about the same size as potatoes for roasting. Lay the pumpkin out on a baking tray and place in medium oven – gas 4/350°F/ 180°C – until soft; this should take about 35 minutes. Remove from the oven, peel and push the pulp through a sieve; alternatively you could use a food processor.

Add the amaretti or ratafia, the pickled fruit or spicy apple chutney, half the Parmesan, the nutmeg, salt, pepper and lemon juice. Mix all these ingredients together very thoroughly.

When the texture is smooth, but fairly stiff, cover with a napkin, and place in the larder or the bottom of the fridge until you are ready to use it.

Now make the pasta itself. Put all the flour, except about 3 oz/75 g, in a pile on the work surface. Make a hole in the centre with your fist and break the eggs into it. Add a pinch of salt and, using both hands, mix the eggs, flour and salt together into a smooth dough. Knead this dough as much as possible – the longer you work it, the smoother and more pliable it will become.

Use the remaining flour to dust the work surface and rolling pin. Roll the dough out very thinly, then fold it all up and roll it again. When it has become really elastic, divide in half. Roll both halves out one last time. Hold them up to the light – if you can see newsprint through them you have rolled enough. You should now have 2 sheets of pasta of about the same size.

Take out the filling and arrange it by the tea-spoonful in rows on 1 sheet. Each lump of filling should be about 2½ in/6 cm away from the next one on all sides. Lay the second sheet of pasta on top of the first one, with the filling sandwiched neatly in between. Using your fingers lightly press down around each lump of filling. This is to prevent any accidents during the cooking, so be sure to do it carefully. Run down the rows of filling with a wavy-edged pastry cutter, first vertically then horizontally. You now have lots of rectangular parcels with pumpkin filling. Check each tortello to be sure that the edges are well sealed and will not permit any of the stuffing to escape when you boil them. Arrange them in neat lines on a tray covered with a napkin and leave to rest for at least 45 minutes in a cool place.

When you are ready to cook the tortelli, heat oven to gas 7/425°F/220°C, then turn it off again. Bring a large pot of salted water to the boil and gently slide in the tortelli, and stir very carefully so as not to break them. Cook for about 5 minutes then drain them. Use a fish slice or slotted spoon to scoop them out rather than pouring them into a colander.

Arrange them in a heated ovenproof dish in layers with melted butter and the remaining Parmesan in between the layers. Put into the hot but unlit oven for 10 minutes to rest before serving.

SPAGHETTI WITH SCALLOPS

SPAGHETTI CON LE PATELLE

CAMPANIA

SERVES 4

4 tablespoons olive oil	salt and pepper
2 cloves garlic, crushed	13 oz/400 g spaghetti
4 tablespoons parsley, chopped	10 oz/300 g scallops, carefully washed and drained (p. 27)
6 canned tomatoes, drained, deseeded and chopped finely	

Remove the roes from the scallops and keep whole, cut the white part in two.

Put a large pot of salted water on to boil while you prepare the sauce. Heat the olive oil in a saucepan with the garlic. As soon as it is brownish, add the parsley and tomatoes, stir and season.

When the salted water is vigorously boiling, put in the spaghetti. Stir well and replace the lid to bring back to the boil quickly. Then remove the lid and cook as normal, stirring occasionally to prevent sticking.

When the spaghetti is half cooked – after about 6 minutes – add the scallops to the tomato sauce. Finish cooking the pasta, then drain it carefully and dress with the sauce. Toss together thoroughly and serve at once.

VESUVIAN FUSILLI

FUSILLI ALLA VESUVIANA

CAMPANIA

SERVES 4

13 oz/400 g fusilli, or any other shape of pasta* (dried variety)	5 tablespoons olive oil
13 oz/400 g fresh ripe tomatoes or equivalent in canned tomatoes	3 oz/75 g pecorino* cheese, grated
4 oz/125 g fresh mozzarella,* cubed	generous pinch of oregano
	salt and pepper

Bring a large saucepan, filled with salted water, to the boil to cook the pasta. Heat the oven to gas 7/425°F/220°C and then turn it off. Toss the pasta into the water, stir to prevent sticking, and leave it to cook while you prepare the sauce. Fusilli take about 15 minutes to cook, but check the instructions on the packet.

Put the tomatoes, chopped and deseeded if using fresh ones, into a saucepan with the mozzarella, olive oil, pecorino, oregano, salt and pepper. Stir it all together over a medium heat, then cover with a lid to simmer gently while the pasta finishes cooking. When the pasta is cooked, drain and transfer to a warm dish, pour over the sauce and toss together. Place in the hot, unlit oven for 5 minutes before serving.

LAGANE AND BEANS

LAGANE E FAGIOLI

BASILICATA-LUCANIA

SERVES 6

1 lb/500 g dried borlotti or
kidney beans, soaked
overnight in cold water

1¼ lb/625 g wide
tagliatelle (the dried
variety)

4 tablespoons olive oil

1 red chilli pepper,
chopped finely

2 cloves garlic, chopped
finely

salt and pepper

Drain and wash the beans. Place in a pot, cover with cold water and bring to the boil. Boil fiercely for 10 minutes, then drain them again. Return beans to pot, cover with fresh water and add 3 pinches of salt. Bring to the boil and simmer for about 30 minutes, or until soft.

Bring a second saucepan full of salted water to the boil, toss in the pasta and stir to prevent sticking. Cook for about 6-7 minutes.

While the tagliatelle (lagane) are cooking, heat the olive oil in a small pan with the chilli and the garlic; allow the garlic to become golden.

Drain the beans and the pasta, transfer to a warm serving bowl and pour over the oil with the garlic and chilli. Season and toss carefully before serving.

ROMAN GNOCCHI WITH SAFFRON

GNOCCHI ALLA ROMANA CON ZAFFERANO

LAZIO

SERVES 4

1¼ pt/750 ml milk

4 oz/125 g butter

8 oz/250 g semolina

3 oz/75 g Parmesan, *
grated

½ teaspoon powdered
saffron

2 oz/50 g Gruyère, grated

salt and pepper

Bring the milk to the boil with 1 tablespoon butter and a pinch of salt. Lower the heat and sprinkle in the semolina. Stir together energetically and continue to cook, stirring constantly, for about 30 minutes. Remove from the heat, stir in 1 tablespoon Parmesan and the saffron and set aside.

Wet a large flat area – the kitchen table is best – and pour out the semolina to form a large disc. Flatten it as much as possible with a knife or spatula and leave to cool.

To form the gnocchi, cut it out with a round cutter into lots of small circles – about 3 in/7 cm across.

To make the dish, melt the remaining butter. Pour a little melted butter into the bottom of an ovenproof dish and arrange a layer of gnocchi on the bottom.

Sprinkle with Parmesan and brush a little butter over this first layer, then cover with more gnocchi and add more butter and Parmesan. Continue in this way until you have used up all the gnocchi. Then cover with Gruyère and grind a little pepper over the top.

Place in a hottish oven, gas 7/425°F/220°C, for about 30 minutes, or until the top has formed a golden crust.

Serve directly from an attractive ovenproof dish with more melted butter, if required.

MILANESE RISOTTO

RISOTTO ALLA MILANESE

LOMBARDY

SERVES 4

4 oz/125 g butter or margarine	2 oz/50 g beef bone marrow
1 large onion, finely chopped	13 oz/400 g risotto* rice
2 sachets powdered saffron or 20 saffron threads	2½ pt/1.5 litres very best meat broth, kept hot
	4 oz/125 g Parmesan,* grated

Melt half the butter in a large heavy-bottomed saucepan, add the onion and fry gently until transparent.

Add the beef marrow – to remove it from the bone, place the bone in a hottish oven for about 3 minutes then slide the marrow out gently – and stir together carefully.

Put the saffron powder or threads to soak in 2 tablespoons of the hot broth.

Add the rice to the pan and toast it lightly for a few minutes, then add the first ladleful of the boiling hot broth, stir it in and simmer. When all the broth is absorbed add another ladleful.

Continue to cook the rice in this way. Never add more broth until the previous ladleful has been absorbed into the rice. It will take 20 minutes to cook the rice. Five minutes before it is cooked, drain the saffron and add the liquid. Stir in very thoroughly.

When the rice is cooked it should be soft to the bite, and the risotto should have a fairly thick, creamy consistency.

Stir in the rest of the butter and the Parmesan, allow the risotto to rest under a lid for 5 minutes, then turn out onto a platter and serve.

SEAFOOD RISOTTO

RISOTTO DE CAPAROZZOLI

VENETO

SERVES 4

2 lb/1 kg assorted molluscs (mussels, clams, scallops, and any others available)	4 tablespoons chopped parsley
5 tablespoons olive oil	13 oz/400 g risotto* rice
2 cloves garlic, finely chopped	2 pt/1.2 litres fish stock, kept very hot
	pepper

Scrub the barnacles and seaweed off the outer shells and wash the molluscs carefully, preferably in sea water, certainly in salted water. Discard any mussels and clams that are open and do not close when tapped firmly.

Put the mussels and clams in a pan and place over a medium heat; shake the pan gently until they have all opened. This should take no more than 7 minutes. Any shells that have not opened after this time are not going to and must be thrown away – do not attempt to force them open as they will be harmful if used.

Remove the molluscs from the shells and set them aside.

Scallops are usually sold open, but in case you need to open them: open scallop shells with a knife, run the knife under the outer rim of the flesh to separate the scallop from the shell. Cut the white muscle and pink roe loose from the other organs, wash and cut the white part in 2 or 3 slices.

Heat the olive oil with the garlic and parsley in another pan and add the shellfish. Cook gently for about 5 minutes, stirring all the time, then add the rice. Toast briefly, then begin adding the hot fish stock, 1 ladleful at a time, until the previous quantity of liquid has been absorbed by the rice. Stir all the time, taking care not to spoil the shellfish.

Season with a little pepper and continue to cook in this way for 20 minutes. When the risotto is ready, the rice will be tender to the bite.

Turn out onto a serving platter, decorate with a few empty shells and serve.

RISOTTO WITH TROUT

RISOTTO CON LE TROTE

VENETO

SERVES 4

2 trout, weighing about 13 oz/400 g together, cleaned and gutted

2 bay leaves

sprig of parsley

½ carrot

½ stick celery

salt

4 oz/125 g butter

2 cloves garlic, crushed

pinch of dried mixed herbs

¼ pt/150 ml dry white wine

13 oz/400 g risotto* rice

Poach the fish in a deep pan with the bay leaves, parsley, carrot, celery and a little salt and water to cover. When the fish are cooked – about 25 minutes – remove them from the stock and set to one side. Strain the stock in the pan and put that aside too.

Skin the fish and remove all the flesh. Flake it carefully, then fry gently in half the butter with the garlic, dried herbs and wine. Mix carefully until the fumes have evaporated, then add the rice. Toast briefly, stirring it in slowly with the fish, then add some of the fish stock and keep stirring.

Cook the risotto for 20 minutes, adding stock as you go along. Don't add more stock until the previous quantity has been absorbed into the rice. Check seasoning before serving.

SPINACH GNOCCHI

GNOCCHI DI SPINACI

LOMBARDY

SERVES 6

1¼ lb/625 g fresh spinach or equivalent frozen

1 small onion, peeled and whole with a deep cut in its flesh

5 oz/150 g butter

8 oz/250 g ricotta,* as fresh as possible, or equivalent weight in soft white bread soaked in milk

5 oz/150 g Parmesan,* grated

pinch of nutmeg

2 eggs

1 egg yolk

8 oz/250 g plain flour

salt and pepper

Wash and pick over the spinach, if using fresh, and cook until tender. Chop very finely. If using frozen spinach, thaw and squeeze out excess water. Fry the whole onion in 1 oz/25 g of the butter for 5 minutes, then remove the onion and put in the spinach. Fry the spinach gently for about 10 minutes, then put aside and allow to cool.

When the spinach is quite cold add the ricotta, half the Parmesan, the nutmeg, eggs and egg yolk, and 7 oz/200 g of flour. Mix all these ingredients together very thoroughly, season with salt and pepper, and then divide into lots of small lumps about the size of ping-pong balls to form the gnocchi. Roll them lightly in flour and then toss them very carefully into a large saucepan of boiling water.

Cook the gnocchi in batches – they are ready as soon as they return to the surface. Scoop them out as they cook, drain well and lay them in an ovenproof dish. Melt the remaining butter and pour it over the gnocchi. Sprinkle with the remaining Parmesan and place in a warm oven for 3 minutes before serving.

POTATO GNOCCHI WITH MEAT AND TOMATO SAUCE

GNOCCHI DI PATATE AL SUGO

PIEDMONT

SERVES 4

2 tablespoons olive oil	salt and pepper
1 onion, chopped	pinch of mixed herbs
1 carrot, chopped	2 lb/1 kg floury potatoes
1 stick celery, chopped	(e.g. Maris Piper)
17 fl oz/500 ml passata*	7 oz/200 g plain flour
8 oz/250 g shin of beef	2 tablespoons butter
or stewing beef, chopped	3 oz/75 g Parmesan,*
finely	grated

To make the sauce, heat the oil in a saucepan, add the onion, carrot and celery and fry gently until soft and the onion transparent, then pour in the passata. Mix together and bring back to a simmer, then add the meat, salt, pepper and herbs. Cook gently for approximately 2 hours, adding a little more passata should it dry out too much.

To make the gnocchi wash the potatoes, but do not peel them, and cook in salted water. When ready, remove the skins quickly while they are still hot. Push them through a mouli before they have a chance to cool, and allow the mashed potato to form a mound on the work surface. Add a little flour to it and knead together with your hands. Continue adding flour and working the mixture with your hands until you have a smooth dough which does not stick to the fingers any more.

Divide the dough into pieces and stretch each one into a long roll about the thickness of your little finger. Cut each roll into pieces about 1 in/2.5 cm long. Take each little piece and roll it with your thumb against the back of a cheese grater or the back of a fork in order to form grooves on one side and a thumb-sized hollow on the other. Keep dusting everything with flour to prevent sticking. Allow the finished gnocchi to fall onto a floured surface and leave them to rest while you bring a very big pot of salted water to the boil. Toss in a few at a time and remove with a draining spoon as soon as they come back up to the surface.

Arrange them in a warm dish when they are cooked. When they are all ready, add the butter and the meat sauce and mix together with extreme care so as not to break the gnocchi. Add the Parmesan and toss once more before serving.

VERMICELLI WITH ANCHOVIES AND GARLIC

VERMICELLI AGLIO E OLIO

CAMPANIA

SERVES 4

13 oz/400 g long vermicelli or spaghetti	*2 tablespoons chopped parsley*
4 tablespoons olive oil	*2 tablespoons fresh white breadcrumbs*
2 cloves garlic, peeled and left whole	*large pinch of red chilli pepper*
4 canned or salted anchovies, cleaned and chopped	*salt*

The sauce of anchovies and garlic cooks in the same amount of time as it takes to cook the vermicelli. If you can't get vermicelli, use ordinary spaghetti.

Put a pan of salted water on to boil to cook the pasta while you get the sauce ready. Heat the oil with the garlic, and remove garlic once browned. Add the anchovies and mix thoroughly with a fork to mash them to a smooth cream. Stir in the parsley and breadcrumbs, then sprinkle in the chilli pepper. Taste, and add salt as required.

When the water comes to the boil, put in the vermicelli and cook for 8-9 minutes. Drain the vermicelli, put into a warmed bowl, pour over the sauce and toss carefully before serving.

TAGLIATELLE WITH PARMA HAM

TAGLIATELLE AL PROSCIUTTO

EMILIA-ROMAGNA

SERVES 6

1 lb/500 g fresh tagliatelle	*pepper*
4 oz/125 g butter	*4 oz/125 g Parmesan,* * *grated*
½ onion, finely chopped	
*7 oz/200 g prosciutto crudo**	

Bring a large pan of salted water to the boil to cook the pasta in. Don't put it in yet as, being fresh, it will take only 2 or 3 minutes to cook.

Meanwhile, melt half the butter in a pan and fry the onion in it very gently. Remove all the fat from the ham and chop it finely, chop the meaty part also and keep it separate. Add the chopped ham fat to the butter and onion, and mix together very carefully. When it has all melted add the rest of the ham and mix together. Season with a little pepper.

Toss the fresh pasta into the boiling water and, as soon as it is cooked, drain it and return to the pan off the heat. Add the remaining butter and half the ham mixture and toss together. Put in half the Parmesan and toss again.

Arrange in a warm serving bowl and make a hollow in the centre of the pasta. Place the remaining ham mixture in the hollow, dust with the rest of the Parmesan and serve at once.

RISOTTO WITH CHICKEN

RISOTTO ALLA SBIRRAGLIA

VENETO

SERVES 4-6

one 2½ lb/1.25 kg chicken, with giblets

1 onion, cut into quarters

1 carrot, cut into quarters

1 stick celery, cut into quarters

salt and pepper

5 tablespoons olive oil

1 onion, finely chopped

1 carrot, finely chopped

1 stick celery, finely chopped

5 oz/150 g lean veal, cut into very small cubes

¼ pt/150 ml dry white wine

14 oz/450 g risotto* rice

6 or 7 tablespoons Parmesan,* grated

Remove the skin from the chicken and cut off as much of the meat as possible. Trim and chop the meat finely. Chop the liver and set to one side with the meat.

Place the carcass and all the remaining parts of the chicken into a large saucepan with 3½ pt/2 litres cold water, the quartered onion, carrot and celery. Season with salt and pepper, and place the pan, with the lid on, over medium heat. Bring to the boil and allow this stock to simmer for approximately 1 hour. Strain and keep warm.

Heat the olive oil in a large heavy-bottomed pan and add to it the finely chopped onion, carrot and celery. Stir carefully together, then put in the veal and all the raw chopped chicken, including the liver. Cook gently until browned, then pour in the wine and place a lid on the pan. Allow to simmer until the chicken is half cooked.

Add the rice and stir very thoroughly. Pour in a ladleful of stock and stay with the risotto, stirring all the time to prevent it sticking. As the rice absorbs the stock, add another ladleful until you have used it up or the rice is cooked. It must become soft and creamy, and this should take 20 minutes.

Season with salt and pepper if required, stir in the Parmesan and serve at once with a bowl containing more Parmesan should anybody wish to add any to their portion.

LOMBARDY

In the 6th century, the Longobards occupied the entire Italian peninsula and it was all called Longobardia. Gradually the name and the area have been further and further reduced until they have reached the present situation where Lombardy is Italy's fourth largest region. And out of every 1,000 Italians 140 live here.

The region lies between the central Alps and the Po River. It occupies the central area of the Pianura Padana with the lovely lake Maggiore to the west and lake Garda to the east. This enormous region with mountains, soft valleys, open plains, lakes and rivers, bustling, busy, rich cities and a wealth of industry and commerce, must surely be the envy of many.

Its massive agricultural production plays a very important part in the region's economy as well as in its gastronomy. Top quality vegetables are produced, thanks to the high limestone content in the fertile soil, rich green pastures produce the best of Italy's beef and veal as well as an enormous wealth of dairy products, and the vine grows absolutely everywhere – on the mountains, in the valleys, by the lakes and on the plains. In fact, so great is the wine production that virtually every village has a wine of its own. And these are indeed excellent wines, praised throughout history by the likes of Virgil, Pliny and Leonardo da Vinci.

The cuisine of Lombardy is a refined, tasty affair using the best quality produce available locally. Regional produce includes rice, which grows prolifically on the fog bound plains; smoked and preserved meats like salame and sausages; rich dairy cream, milk, butter and cheeses of many kinds; excellent beef and veal.

Everything in Lombardy is cooked to suit the demands and tastes of people who are certainly living in one of the world's most important commercial centres. Although the Lombard has the reputation for being too busy making money, in too much of a hurry striking yet another deal to sit down and enjoy his food, and although the unkind have said that most of the region's specialities have been created in order to combine first and second courses and thus save time and money (such as, for example, casêula, or ossobuco with risotto), when it comes to serious eating even the most dedicated Milanese business-man takes a holiday and becomes human at table! Whatever you eat in Lombardy, even the simplest sandwich will be of superbly high quality, as this is a region where the people demand the best of every-thing.

The local specialities include world renowned Minestrone; Cotoletta alla Milanese – a fine slice of veal tossed in egg and breadcrumbs and then fried in butter; delicious saffron yellow risotto; the richly satisfying Stufato – a joint of beef cooked slowly with tomatoes and other vegetables; a type of pickled fruit called Mostarda di Cremona; and the airy Christmas cake called Panettone, which changes into a dove shape for Easter and is then called Colomba.

The cheeses of Lombardy are gorgonzola, strac-chino, taleggio, bel paese, groviera and the king and queen of cream cheeses – mascarpone and robiola. Mascarpone is very often served with pears as a deli-cious dessert.

There are so many wonderful wines to be savoured in Lombardy that I have only mentioned my personal favourites. Sassella is a bright ruby red wine with a bouquet of roses. It is perfect for drinking with rare game and rare red meat. Chiaretto del Garda is a lovely pale pink wine with a bouquet of almonds and a lovely nutty taste. I often serve it as an aperitif, but it also goes very well with roasts, par-ticularly roast poultry. Barbagallo and Buttafuoco are two lovely soft, mellow, rich red wines that are perfect for sipping slowly on cold winter evenings. Finally, Moscato di Casteggio is a delicate, slightly sparkling yellow wine with a lovely sweet flavour that is an excellent dessert wine.

PIEDMONT

Approach Piedmont's delicious collection of dishes with your senses prepared, for every dish has a strong sensual appeal, wonderfully pungent smells and rich colours. Food and drink are taken seriously in Piedmont; there is a deeply felt dignity and sobriety which accompanies the preparation and consumption of its regional dishes. The techniques are not unlike those used in France, but with a smaller measure of finesse. Vegetables are often served raw with a garlic dressing, the bread is always brown and seems to keep for days on end. The wines are famous all over the world for being hearty, wholesome and strong, even their names reflect their nature – Barbera, Barbaresco, Gattinara. Butter, fresh from the herds which graze in the hillside pastures, is used liberally in everything to dress and moisten.

The name Piedmont means 'at the foot of the mountains', and it is exactly so. The region lies in the upper Po valley, embraced by the arc of the central and western Alps. The valleys descend like spokes of a wheel towards the 'basse', the low plains around Novara and Vercelli where the many waterways are channelled into irrigation for the rice and grain crops.

Further south the plains are broken up by the smooth hills of Monferrato and the Langhe, which are reminiscent of parts of Tuscany with their tranquil, vine-clad slopes.

The pastures of Piedmont are lush, crops flourish, the orchards and vineyards are filled with fruit – and all this in a region which is mainly famed for its industrial economy. Only in Piedmont will you find paddy fields alongside Fiat factories.

The cooking of these parts appears to be predominantly prepared for the hearty appetites of strong, hungry, outdoor men. The people here are used to hard work and cold weather. Highly seasoned dishes and rich roasts are popular, but France is not far off and her influence is felt in many subtle combinations of cream cheese, cream and butter. The town and province of Alba produces white truffles to be shredded lightly onto pasta, over a risotto or served with turkey breasts fried lightly in butter. There is solid yellow polenta to eat with substantial stews, the famous Bollito, a collection of boiled meats served hot with a wonderful emerald green sauce. There are partridges, pheasants, haunches of venison roasted over open fires, deep yellow peaches, often stuffed and baked, chestnuts, chocolate, confectionery, and many other delights of which Piedmont can rightfully feel proud.

It is worth mentioning just a few of Piedmont's famous wines. Grignolino has a light and charming bouquet with a deliciously nutty flavour. Much improved with ageing, it has a clear brilliant garnet colour. Sweet Nebbiolo is a delicate red dessert wine which acquires a lovely pinkish colour, shot through with golden lights as it ages. Barolo has a faint bouquet of violets and is a red wine which starts out being fairly harsh and coarse, but it mellows to become velvety smooth as it ages. It takes its place on the list of the finest wines produced in Italy. Barbera is a dark ruby wine; plenty of body with a genuine tonic quality about it. You can really taste the vine! The bouquet is very faintly reminiscent of cherries.

LIGURIA

The Ligurian cook is fast, quick thinking and independent. That which does not grow and is not available in Liguria is quite simply ignored and therefore rarely appears on the menu. As Liguria does not have wide pastures and herds of fat cattle for the production of butter and cream these ingredients are very rarely used, and when they are it is with a somewhat suspicious air – as though they haven't as yet been really accepted as official ingredients for cooking with.

In Liguria, everything that grows or blooms is used in the cooking. Apart from the carnation, which as far as I know has not yet been put into any dish, everything under the Ligurian sun will sooner or later end up in the pot. Garlic characterizes the region's good flavours, borage and basil tinge everything with green and there is the most amazing olive oil which is used in everything – even the cakes!

Ligurians have a reputation for being mean, but it is rather an ability to make the most of everything around them. For example, take pesto, Liguria's most famous speciality; it is an unlikely combination of ingredients when seen on paper, but the Ligurians found olives, basil, walnuts and garlic growing in the same place and so they pounded them together to create a delicious, creamy, green sauce with which to dress hot pasta.

All the herbs of the garden are used to create the Ligurian pasta dough. This sfoglia is not the deep golden, rich pasta dough of Emilia-Romagna, nor the heavy sfoglia of Lombardy and Piedmont. Here they make it white, speckled with green from the chopped herbs – then cut finely to make the superb trenette verdi.

Liguria has no mozzarella of its own, but no attempt is made to start competing in dishes which require it – like pizza for instance. Instead of a copy of a Neapolitan pizza, they create their own – a wonderful pizza invented by the famous Admiral Andrea Doria and named after him: 'pizza all'Andrea' or 'pizzalandrea' or 'pissadella'. And then there are the fragrant white pizzas with local cheese oozing out from inside or covered with a layer of sweet onions.

And of course, last but by no means least there is the fish of the blue Ligurian sea which is all used, right down to the last scale – this is the secret of the

Ligurian fish soup, Ciuppin, which will only come out right if a sufficient variety of fish is used. Fish is everywhere, from the Burrida – a quick fish stew made with fresh vegetables and tomatoes – to a cold whitebait and saffron salad, from the enormous variety of recipes for seafood and the octopus specialities to the vast dentex which swims these rocky shores and ends up on the table in a thousand different ways.

The boundaries of this region are the upper part of the Tyrrhenian sea, which is called the Ligurian sea, the Maritime Alps – with the Appenines dividing them to the north and north east from Piedmont to Emilia-Romagna; to the east lies Tuscany and the River Magra. The main tourist attraction of the region are the two rivieras. The vegetation grows thick and luxurious amongst the villas in the pretty seaside towns.

The wines seem to have all been made especially to go with the fish dishes and savoury pies that are served here. Well worth trying are the golden yellow Cinqueterre wines, with very aromatic bouquets; even though the area of production consists only of five tiny villages, the flavour can vary enormously from bottle to bottle. They are excellent wines with a fine, delicate flavour and a sharp undertone. Look out also for the slightly sweet Coronata with a lovely straw yellow colour and a delicate light bouquet. To drink with soups and heavy foods there is the lovely ruby red Dolceacqua, a generous wine with a very distinctive, slightly sweet flavour and a rich bouquet. Portofino is a clear, lemon-yellow wine with a sharp, dry, tart flavour which can be drunk with anything. Serve it very cold. Vermentino is a pale yellow very dry wine which is slightly sparkling and boasts a good bouquet. Served chilled it is very refreshing and is best with desserts or fish. Finally, try the Polcevera with a dry nutty taste that tends to sweetness and has a faint, delicate bouquet. Of a light straw yellow colour, it is served with fish dishes.

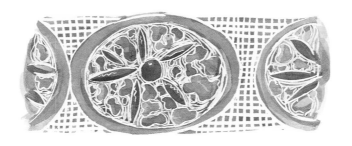

3
PIZZA, EGG AND CHEESE DISHES

VEGETABLE PIZZA

PIZZA DI VERDURA

APULIA

SERVES 4

1½ oz/40 g fresh yeast or	4 tablespoons olive oil
¾ oz/20 g dried yeast	2 oz/50 g black olives,
13 oz/400 g plain flour	stoned and finely chopped
salt and pepper	2 oz/50 g capers, washed
2½ lb/1.25 kg radicchio	and finely chopped
1 large clove garlic, peeled	1 egg, beaten

Prove the yeast in a little warm water to make a smooth paste. Put the flour onto the work surface in a mound and make a hole in the centre with your fist. Pour the yeast mixture into the hole, add a pinch each of salt and pepper and enough warm water to start kneading.

Work the dough thoroughly to create a very smooth texture. Put the dough in an oiled bowl under a tea cloth and leave to rise in a warm place for about 2 hours.

Clean the radicchio, wash it carefully, then dry it and chop it coarsely. Place it in a saucepan with the garlic and half the oil. Season and allow to cook gently under a lid for 15 minutes. Leave it to cool until the dough is ready to use.

When the dough is well risen, divide it into 2 balls. Roll out half of the dough to line an oiled flan tin and fill with the cooked radicchio. Scatter the olives and capers over the radicchio, then cover with the other half of the dough. Carefully seal the edges of the pizza by pinching together with finger and thumb all the way around. Brush with the beaten egg. Place in a preheated oven, gas 4/350°F/180°C for 30 minutes.

Allow to cool before serving cold as a snack or starter or main course. This is also an original and delicious dish to take on picnics.

RED ONION PIZZA

FITASCETTA

LOMBARDY

SERVES 4-6

1 lb/500 g red onions, thinly sliced

2 oz/50 g butter

2 tablespoons olive oil

pinch of salt

2 tablespoons sugar

10 oz/300 g bread dough, ready-made – can be prepared with a mix, or as for Vegetable Pizza (p. 36)

Cook the onions very slowly and carefully in the butter and half the olive oil. They should stew gently for about 1 hour. When they are cooked, add salt and set aside. Roll out the bread dough like a long thick sausage. Oil a round cake tin and coil the bread dough in it, leaving a hole in the centre as big as possible. Press the dough carefully into position, then spread the cooked onions over it as evenly as you can. Sprinkle with the sugar and bake in a moderate oven, gas 5/375°F/190°C, for 30 minutes. The result is an extremely fragrant, flattish pizza with a hole in the middle. It is eaten hot as a snack or as an antipasto.

CHEESE FRITTERS

FRITTELLINE DI FORMAGGIO D'AOSTA

PIEDMONT

SERVES 4

7 oz/200 g fontina cheese (if unobtainable, use mature Edam or Gouda or Lancashire)

7 oz/200 g fresh breadcrumbs

2 eggs

4 oz/125 g cooked beef or chicken, minced finely

pinch of mixed spice

½ teaspoon dried mixed herbs

3 tablespoons milk

salt and pepper

oil for deep frying

Chop the cheese into tiny squares or grate it thickly and mix it with the breadcrumbs, eggs, meat, spice, herbs and milk. Mix until you have a fairly even texture, then season to taste. Heat the oil in the deep fryer until sizzling and spoon the mixture in, a spoonful at a time. Cook quickly on both sides – about 4 minutes altogether – then scoop out and drain on kitchen paper. Serve the frittelline hot as a main course with spinach cooked in butter, or as a starter on their own.

DROWNED OMELETTE

FRITTATA AFFOGATA

TUSCANY

SERVES 4

5 eggs	1 onion, chopped
salt and pepper	4 sprigs parsley, chopped
1 teaspoon plain flour	6 large fresh basil leaves, chopped
1 heaped teaspoon fresh breadcrumbs	
	3 tablespoons olive oil
4 tablespoons oil for frying	10 oz/300 g passata* or canned tomatoes,* sieved to remove seeds and reduced to a smooth purée
1 large stick celery, chopped finely	

Beat the eggs thoroughly with the salt and pepper, flour and breadcrumbs. Heat the frying oil in a largish pan and when it sizzles pour in the egg mixture.

Shaking the pan and, lifting the edges, cook on one side for about 5 minutes. Then slide the omelette onto a lid or plate the same size as the pan and turn it over, slipping it back into the pan on the other side.

Cook for another 5 minutes, then slide the omelette onto kitchen paper to drain and cool. When the omelette is cool, slice it into strips about the size of a finger.

Meanwhile, combine the celery, onion, parsley and basil and heat the olive oil in another saucepan. Cook the herbs and vegetables in the oil until the onion is transparent, then pour in the tomatoes and mix together. Season and simmer for about 30 minutes.

Stir in the strips of omelette and serve hot as a main course with a salad.

Drowned Omelette is also an excellent dish to take, cold, on a picnic.

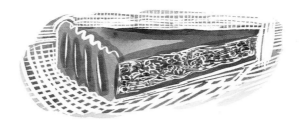

WHITE PIZZA WITH CHEESE

FOCACCIA AL FORMAGGIO

LIGURIA

SERVES 6

4 fl oz/125 ml virgin olive oil	8 oz/250 g Gruyère, diced
7 oz/200 g strong white flour	4 oz/125 g mozzarella, * diced
salt	

Work almost all the oil into the flour with cold water until you have kneaded a smooth and soft dough. Place it in an oiled bowl and keep in a warm, draught-free place for 1 hour. Knead again, and then let it rest on the floured work surface for 5 minutes before rolling it into a large circle, as wide and as thin as you can – in Liguria they use a baking tin with a diameter of at least 20 in/50 cm – then cut it in 2.

Place one semicircle on an oiled baking tray or a large oiled baking tin and press it down carefully with oiled hands. Spread the cheese all over the surface, then cover with the other sheet of dough. Oil it all over and seal the edges carefully, then use a pointed knife to make holes in it about the size of a 10 pence piece. You should make about 10 holes all over the focaccia.

Bake in a very hot oven, gas 9/475°F/240°C, for 6 minutes or until crisp and golden. Slice and serve at once as a snack or starter.

TROUSERS-STUFFED PIZZA DOUGH

CALZONE

CAMPANIA

SERVES 4

7 oz/200 g ricotta*	4 oz/125 g Neapolitan salame* or prosciutto, * chopped
1 egg	
pinch of salt	1 1/4 lb/575 g bread dough, ready-made (p. 38)
4 tablespoons Parmesan, * grated	2 tablespoons olive oil
4 oz/125 g mozzarella, * cubed	

Sieve the ricotta into a bowl, put in the egg and mix carefully. Add the salt, Parmesan, mozzarella and salame or prosciutto, then mix it all together.

Oil the work surface lightly and flatten out the bread dough on it in a large circle about 1/4 in/5 mm thick. Spread the ricotta mixture over half the dough, and especially in the centre. Fold the dough in half and press the edges together, sealing the calzone like an envelope. Place on an oiled baking tray and put into a hot oven, gas 6/400°F/200°C, for 30 minutes.

Serve hot as a snack, or as a starter, or even a main course. The same procedure goes for making 4 individual calzoni. As an alternative filling use chopped spinach and ricotta.

CALABRIAN PIZZA

PITTA CHICCULIATA

CALABRIA

SERVES 4-6

1 lb 5 oz/650 g plain flour

1½ oz/40 g fresh yeast, proved in a little warm water to make a smooth paste

salt and pepper

2 lb/1 kg passata* or canned tomatoes,* sieved to remove all seeds and reduced to a smooth purée

8 tablespoons olive oil

2 cloves garlic, crushed

4 oz/125 g lard

3 egg yolks

9 oz/275 g canned tuna fish in oil, flaked

2 oz/50 g capers, washed and chopped

2 oz/50 g black olives, washed and chopped

Pour out the flour onto the work surface, make a hole in the centre with your fist and pour the yeast mixture into the hole. Add a pinch of salt. Work the yeast into the flour adding warm water, as required, to make a fairly soft dough. Put the dough in an oiled bowl, cover with a tea cloth and leave in a warm place to rise until it has doubled in size, about 2 hours.

Place the sieved tomatoes in a saucepan with 4 tablespoons olive oil and the garlic, season and simmer for about 20 minutes, stirring occasionally. Remove from the heat and leave to cool.

Put the dough back onto the work surface and slap it lightly with your hands to cause most of the air to escape. Make a hollow in the centre and place in it three quarters of the lard and 2 egg yolks. Work them into the dough very thoroughly with a pinch of pepper. When the dough is well kneaded, remove one third of it and set it aside.

Roll out the larger ball of dough into a large disc. Oil a flan tin with a diameter of about 10 in/25 cm, and line the bottom and sides with the large disc of dough. Fill it with the tomato mixture into which you have stirred the tuna, capers and olives. Roll out the remaining piece of dough to a circle large enough to cover the top and seal the edges very carefully by folding them over on top of one another. Rub the surface over with the rest of the lard and brush well with the remaining egg yolk. Place in a warm place to rise again for 30 minutes. Bake in a hot oven, gas 4/350°F/180°C, for 25-30 minutes and serve hot as a starter or main course.

Toasted Mozzarella and Anchovies

CROSTINI DI MOZZARELLA E ALICI

LAZIO

SERVES 4

10 oz/300 g mozzarella*

1 small baguette or similar crusty loaf

salt and pepper

6 oz/175 g butter

2 canned anchovies, cleaned and chopped finely

4 tablespoons warm milk

Slice the mozzarella and the bread into slices of the same size and in equal proportions. Thread alternate slices of bread and mozzarella onto metal skewers, making sure they are close together and very firmly attached. Sprinkle with a little salt and pepper. Lay the skewers across a roasting tin so that the cheese and bread are suspended in mid air, supported by the skewer resting on either side of the tin. (Whenever possible use an outdoor grill to make this dish.) Place the roasting tin in a preheated oven at gas 6/400°F/200°C. Allow the crostini to cook for 20 minutes, basting every so often with 3 oz/75 g melted butter.

Fry the anchovies in the remaining butter to make a sauce; stir in the milk at the last minute. Remove the crostini from the oven, lay them out on a warmed platter and pour the anchovy sauce over them. Serve the crostini hot as a snack or starter, or as a barbecue dish.

Potato Pizza

PIZZA DI PATATE

APULIA

SERVES 4

2 lb/1 kg floury potatoes (e.g. Maris Piper), scrubbed and washed, but not peeled

6 tablespoons olive oil

7 fresh or canned tomatoes, chopped coarsely

1 large onion, thickly sliced

4 canned anchovies, filleted and chopped

4 oz/125 g black olives, stoned and chopped

4 oz/125 g capers, washed and chopped

salt and pepper

Boil the potatoes and quickly peel them while they are still hot. Mash them very thoroughly with salt and pepper and 1 tablespoonful of olive oil. Put the potato mixture aside and fry the onion in another 2 tablespoonfuls of olive oil until the onion is soft but not brown. Add the tomatoes to the onion and cook together for 20 minutes. Oil a round ovenproof dish about 7 in/18 cm in diameter. Spread half the potato mixture very thickly over the bottom. Scatter onto the potato mixture the anchovies, olives, capers and tomato and onion mixture. Season lightly, then cover with the rest of the potato mixture, brush with the remaining oil and place in a hot oven, gas 6/400°F/200°C, for 20 minutes before serving hot as a snack or starter.

COURGETTE OMELETTE

FRITTATA DI ZUCCHINE

TUSCANY

SERVES 4

6 eggs	1 onion, thinly sliced
salt and pepper	2 tablespoons olive oil
6 courgettes, medium-sized, washed and diced	3 tablespoons oil for frying

Beat the eggs until well mixed together with a little salt and pepper. Cook the courgettes gently in a pan with the onion and the olive oil, season with care and allow to cook, turning occasionally, until soft but not mushy. Cool the courgettes and then add them to the egg mixture. Beat again to combine thoroughly.

Heat the oil for frying in an 8 in/20 cm frying pan until really hot. Pour the egg and courgettes into the pan spreading the mixture out evenly with a spatula. Shake the pan and lift the edges of the mixture to allow it to cook on the first side, and about halfway through the thickness of the omelette.

After about 6 minutes turn the omelette upside-down onto a lid or plate of the same size as the pan, and then carefully slide it back into the pan on the uncooked side. Cook for a further 6-7 minutes, again shaking the pan to avoid sticking.

Turn out onto a dish and serve hot or cold, as a starter or as a main course with a mixed salad.

ONION OMELETTE

FRITTATA DI CIPOLLE

ABRUZZO-MOLISE

SERVES 4

6 eggs	salt and pepper
4 large onions, thinly sliced	3 tablespoons oil for frying
3 tablespoons olive oil	

Beat the eggs together very thoroughly. Cook the onions gently in the olive oil until they are soft but not too mushy. Season and cool. Mix into the eggs.

Heat the frying oil until it is really sizzling and pour the egg and onion mixture into the hot pan, and shake it to avoid sticking. Lift the edges of the omelette to help it to cook. When it has fried for about 6 minutes, turn it upside-down onto a lid or plate of the same size as the pan and slide it back into the pan on the other side to finish cooking. Cook for a further 6 minutes before turning out onto a dish.

Serve hot or cold, as a starter or as a main course with salad or vegetables.

EMILIA-ROMAGNA

Without question one of the best gastronomic regions of Italy, this is the fatherland of the inimitable tortellini and all other manner of hand-made pasta, from tagliatelle to the wide yellow sheets of lasagne. The most famous of all Italian cooks, Pellegrino Artusi, said of Emilia-Romagna: 'When you hear Bolognese cooking mentioned, drop a little curtsey, for it deserves it.' It is a some-what heavy cuisine, because the climate requires it to be so, but nowhere else will you find such succu-lent flavours and marvellous textures. It is also wholesome and healthy – octogenarians and nonagerians abound in Emilia-Romagna!

Emilia-Romagna nestles cosily between six reg-ions and lies next to the tiny Republic of San Marino, which separates it from the Marche. It has a long coastline which includes the famous resort of Rimini, a long mountain range which runs on into Tuscany and is called the Appennino Tosco-Emiliano, fertile hills where you will find the odd abandoned castle and tiny remote villages, and from the hills to the coastline the flat, fertile lowlands give the region its excellent agricultural produce. West of Bologna is the city of Parma where Parmesan cheese and Parma ham come from, and no less a gourmet's paradise than Bologna. Worth a mention is the beautiful town of Ravenna, which has a mar-vellous collection of mosaics. Comacchio, rather like Venice, is a town made up of waterways running across the island.

Top of the list of local delicacies and traditional dishes must be the inimitable Bolognese sauce, a delightful concoction of about 15 ingredients which bubble slowly on the stove for hours and hours before being spooned over piping hot home-made pasta. Home-made pasta is made with 100 g of plain flour and one egg per person – the question is, 'How many eggs' worth shall I make for lunch today?' The egg must have a brown shell to make the real thing, and expertise, energy and patience are required to make pasta like they make it here. Once the sfoglia is made, it can be cut and shaped to create stuffed pasta like ravioli, tortellini and capelletti, or broad or nar-row ribbons like lasagne, canelloni, tagliatelle, fet-tuccine, quadrucci, capelli d'angelo and so on. A speciality of the Adriatic coast is the delicious Fritto Misto – all kinds of the freshest fish available, from mullet to squid, sprinkled with flour and fried in boiling hot oil until crisp. Salame, sausages and hams abound, the queen of them all being the enormous mortadella. Stuffed pig's trotter, the pride of Modena, is served on New Year's Eve along with cotechino and lentils. The list is truly endless!

Wine production is not enormous but what there is very good. The most famous local wine is Lam-brusco which comes from many fine vineyards. The four best are Lambrusco di Castelvetro, Lambrusco Grasparossa, Lambrusco Salamino and the best one of all is Lambrusco di Sorbara. Trebbiano is one of the most attractive dry white wines in the entire country and is the most typical wine of the area of Faenza and Forli.

TUSCANY

The happiest days of my life were spent in Tuscany and I shall always have those to thank for my love of cooking. As a child I would peep round the door of the kitchen to see what was going on and instead of being shooed out I would be beckoned in and asked to shell peas, clean lettuce or slice tomatoes, my elbows firmly planted on that lovely marble table watching with wide-eyed wonder as the meal took shape. Then, when the meal was finally served that evening, I would feel an enormous wave of pride wash over me as I knew I had had a part in the preparation. Unforgettable times, in an unforgettable place ...

A heart-shaped region with a little court of perfect islands, a long smooth coastline, mountains, lakes, rivers and an incredible cultural heritage. Apart from its natural beauty and its wealth of cottage industries, many now organised on a modern basis, Tuscany has a flourishing agricultural economy, based on the production of grain and the finest olive oil, forage and stock-breeding: Florentine steaks are famous the world over. But one cannot consider Tuscany's agricultural economy without mentioning Chianti which comes from the province of Siena. Not all Tuscan wine is Chianti wine, only that which is produced there, although neighbouring areas also produce excellent varieties.

Tuscany has succeeded in giving refinement and subtlety to the most ordinary dishes. Living in the middle of so much beauty and history has kept the Tuscan to the straight and narrow when it comes to the aesthetics of cooking. The basic materials here are so good – incomparable olive oil, tender meat, excellent wine; are these enough to explain the superiority of the cuisine which is one of Tuscany's proudest boasts?

Even in a chic city restaurant, the food has a rustic air about it. The delicious soups of vegetables, beans and meat will be brought to your table still bubbling in terracotta pots. Whenever possible, the Tuscan cook will use the spit, the open grill, the log-fired bread oven. Tuscan bread is unsalted, an insipid loaf, baked in this way to allow you to enjoy all the flavours of your meal. A unique invention is the delicious Fagioli al Fiasco, beans cooked in a wine flask so that none of their flavour or texture be lost, then dressed with virgin olive oil and black pepper.

There is also the wealth of fish and seafood, best illustrated by the Cacciucco alla Livornese – a fish stew flavoured with red wine and spices that depends entirely for its success on the availability of the correct fish.

Amongst the wines worth tasting is Aleatico, the speciality of the island of Elba, doubtless used to soothe Napoleon from time to time; it has a faintly liqueurish taste and a deep ruby red colour. Candia, both red and white, are wines with a rather sweet taste that come from the rugged terraces of the Tyrrhenian coast – superb dessert wines that can also marry well with cheese. Brunello di Montalcino is a brilliant garnet red wine with a faint bouquet of violets and a really dry flavour; it improves a great deal with ageing.

From the pretty little town of San Gimignano comes Vernaccia, a golden yellow wine which is brilliantly clear and has a sharp refreshing flavour and a lingering after-taste. Finally, a favourite of mine, the delightful vin santo Toscano with its wonderful amber colour. It is produced on all the best farms throughout the regions by simply pressing grapes that have been left to dry out in the sun. The fermentation is a long, slow process and it takes up to four years for the wine to age properly. The best quality wine is always kept by the producer himself, who distributes glasses of it as a sign of great favour. It is often served at the end of a meal with a plate of Cantucci, knobbly almond biscuits which are dipped in the wine and eaten by the hundred – once you start you cannot stop!

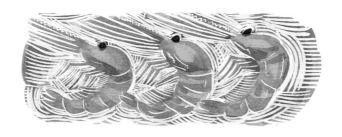

4
FISH DISHES

MACKEREL WITH PEAS

LAXERTI CON I PUISCI

LIGURIA

SERVES 4

3 tablespoons olive oil

1½ lb/750 g mackerel

1 onion, finely chopped

fistful of parsley, finely chopped

4 leaves fresh mint, finely chopped

salt and pepper

10 oz/300 g fresh or frozen peas

5 tablespoons passata* or canned tomatoes* sieved to remove seeds and reduced to a smooth purée

Heat the oil in a wide deep frying pan and add the cleaned and gutted mackerel. Brown them gently on both sides and season with salt and pepper. Sprinkle the onion, parsley and mint over the fish, then add the peas, cover with a lid, and cook for about 10 minutes. Pour over the puréed tomatoes and continue to cook for a further 10-15 minutes. Serve hot.

FISH STEW

STUFATO DI PESCE

LOMBARDY

SERVES 4

7 oz/200 g baby onions, chopped

7 oz/200 g baby carrots, chopped

1½ lb/750 g firm-fleshed fish (thick cod steaks, halibut steaks or salmon)

2 sticks celery, chopped

3 oz/75 g butter

3 tablespoons plain flour

6 fl oz/175 ml dry white wine

salt and pepper

Place the onions, carrots and celery in a saucepan with the butter and cook gently, stirring constantly until the vegetables are soft. Toss the fish, cut into chunks about 3 in/7 cm square, in the flour and add to the vegetables. Turn quickly to brown and seal on all sides, then add the wine and cook quickly without a lid for 3 minutes to evaporate the alcohol. Add

46

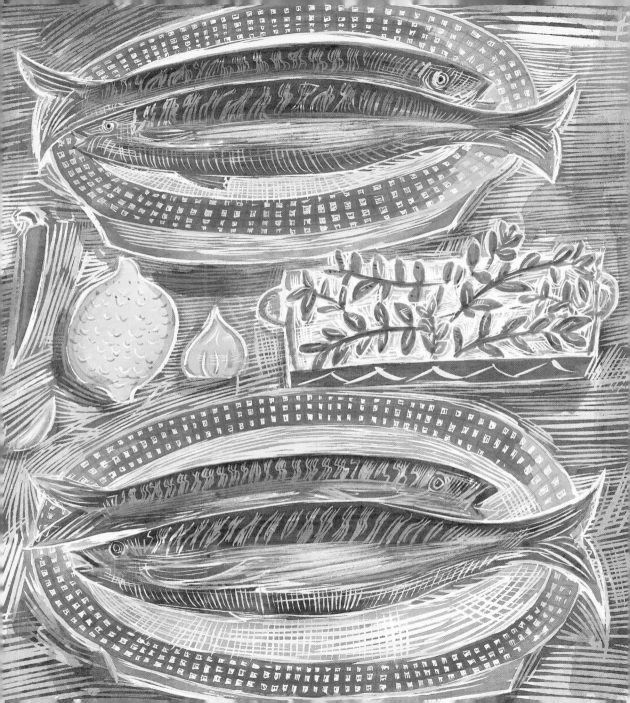

5-6 tablespoons water and continue to cook very gently for about 30 minutes.

Remove the fish from the saucepan and arrange on a warmed serving platter. Sieve the sauce, pour over the fish and serve at once.

WHITEBAIT WITH SAFFRON

PUPPIDDI IN SCAPECE

APULIA

SERVES 4

1 lb/500 g whitebait, washed and dried carefully	salt
	4 tablespoons white wine vinegar
5 tablespoons plain flour	½ teaspoon powdered saffron
oil for deep frying	
4 tablespoons fresh breadcrumbs	

Toss the whitebait in flour and fry them quickly and carefully in the deep fryer. Drain on kitchen paper and then place them in a bowl. Cover with the breadcrumbs and season with salt. Mix the vinegar and saffron together and pour over the fish.

Leave to marinate for about 4 hours in the refrigerator before serving chilled as a starter, or as an accompanying dish with other fish.

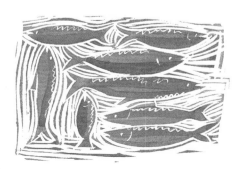

SWORDFISH STEAKS WITH STUFFING

BRACIOLE DI PESCE SPADA

SICILY

SERVES 4

1 large onion, chopped finely	1 heaped tablespoon capers, washed and chopped
1 clove garlic, chopped finely	4 oz/125 g provolone cheese, diced (if unobtainable, use mature Cheddar)
2 oz/50 g trimmings from the swordfish steaks (listed below)	
6 tablespoons olive oil	salt
6 leaves of fresh basil, chopped	pinch of red chilli pepper
fistful of fresh parsley, chopped	2 tablespoons pine kernels
	2 tablespoons sultanas
4 oz/125 g toasted fresh breadcrumbs	8 oz/250 g swordfish, cut into 4 very thin steaks

To make the stuffing, fry the onion, garlic and fish trimmings very gently in 3 tablespoons oil. When the onion is transparent, put in the basil, parsley, breadcrumbs and capers. Mix together thoroughly and cook for about 15 minutes. Blend or sieve this mixture and add the cheese, salt, chilli powder, pine kernels and sultanas. Stir it all together carefully and set it aside. Flatten out the swordfish steaks as much as possible with a meat mallet and put an equal amount of stuffing in the middle of each one. Roll up the swordfish steaks and push a couple of wooden toothpicks through each one to keep them firmly closed. Place in an oiled baking dish, side by side, and sprinkle with any remaining oil. Bake in a hottish oven, gas 6/400°F/200°C, for about 30 minutes before serving.

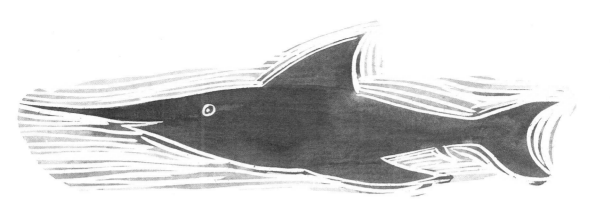

SCAMPI IN HERB SAUCE

SCAMPI IN BUSARA

FRIULI-VENEZIA GIULIA

SERVES 4

1 lb 10 oz/800 g unpeeled scampi	8 tablespoons dry white wine
6 tablespoons olive oil	¼ teaspoon paprika
fistful of mixed fresh basil, marjoram and parsley, finely chopped	salt
	4 cloves garlic, peeled but left whole

Wash and dry the scampi carefully. Heat the oil in a heavy-bottomed pan and add the cloves of garlic to it as soon as it begins to smoke. Fry the garlic until brown, then throw it away and add the scampi. Stir once to cook the scampi on all sides, then add the chopped herbs and stir again. Pour in the wine and bring to the boil. Allow to bubble for 2 or 3 minutes, then season with paprika and salt, stir and cover with a lid. Cook over a lively heat for about 10 minutes then serve as a starter or with other fish dishes as part of the main course.

NEAPOLITAN SARDINES

SARDE ALLA NAPOLETANA

CAMPANIA

SERVES 4

1½ lb/750 g fresh sardines	6 canned tomatoes,* cut in half, seeds removed and then chopped
8 tablespoons olive oil	
salt and pepper	fistful of fresh parsley, chopped finely
large pinch of oregano	
3 cloves garlic, crushed	1 clove garlic, chopped very finely

Gut the fish and remove the heads, then wash and dry carefully.

Pour half the oil into an ovenproof dish and arrange the fish in a row, side by side, in the oil. Sprinkle with salt and pepper, oregano and the crushed garlic. Scatter the tomatoes over the fish, then cover with the parsley and chopped garlic, mixed together. Dribble the remaining oil over the dish and place in a hot oven, gas 6/400°F/200°C, for 20 minutes.

This delicious dish can be served hot or cold.

49

HUSS PIE WITH COURGETTES

IMPANATA DI PALOMBO

SICILY

SERVES 6

1 large onion, finely chopped	1 tablespoon capers, washed and chopped
10 tablespoons olive oil	13 oz/400 g huss, diced
1 stick celery	salt and pepper
2 oz/50 g green olives, stoned and chopped	4 large courgettes, diced
	2 eggs, beaten
8 tablespoons passata* or canned tomatoes,* sieved and reduced to seedless purée	4 tablespoons plain flour
	1 lb/500 g frozen shortcrust pastry, defrosted

Fry the onion in one third of the olive oil with the celery, olives and capers. When the onion is transparent stir in the passata. Cook for 5 minutes, then add the fish. Season, using more pepper than salt as the olives and capers are salty, cover with a lid and simmer gently for 10 minutes. Set aside.

Toss the courgettes in half the beaten egg, then in the flour. Heat the remaining oil until sizzling and fry the courgettes until brown and crisp on the outside. Drain them on kitchen paper and set aside.

Roll out the pastry as thinly as possible and line a 9 in/23 cm pie dish with it. Keep enough pastry to cover the pie. Cover the bottom of the pie dish with half the fish mixture, add the courgettes in one layer and then cover with the rest of the fish. Flatten it down gently with the back of a spoon. Roll out the rest of the pastry for the lid. Put it over the top and seal the edges carefully. Brush with the remaining egg and bake in a moderate oven, gas 2/300°F/150°C for 45 minutes. The top should be crisp and golden. Serve hot as a main course.

VENETIAN SQUID

SEPPIE ALLA VENEZIANA

VENETO

SERVES 4

2 lb/1 kg fresh or frozen squid	6 tablespoons dry white wine, preferably Venetian
1 clove garlic, chopped finely	3 tablespoons tomato purée*
1 small onion, chopped finely	2 ladlefuls fish or chicken stock, kept hot
5 tablespoons olive oil	salt and pepper
fistful of fresh parsley, chopped finely	

First clean the squid unless you are lucky enough to have bought them ready cleaned.

Peel off the outer skin from the entire squid. Separate the head, which also includes the tentacles, from the body, which is shaped like a sack. Slide out the bone carefully without splitting the sack and throw it away – this bone is oval and flat. Using a pair of scissors cut open the sack and open it up like a book. Cut out the black bag of liquid and throw it away but keep the yellow bag of liquid intact as this will add flavour to the dish. Finally remove the sharp beak and the eyes from the head. It is wise to clean squid, or indeed any type of fish, on the draining board as you will need to run the fish and your hands under the tap continuously – this is a very messy job.

Having cleaned the squid, slice them lengthways into neat strips. Do this on a firm chopping board with a very sharp knife. Fry the garlic and onion in the oil until the onion is transparent, then add the parsley and the squid including the tentacles.

Mix together carefully and cook until the squid are golden in colour. Add the wine and boil to evaporate the fumes for 3 minutes before adding the tomato purée, the stock and some of the liquid from the squid if you wish. Stir carefully, cover and simmer gently for 30 minutes. When the squid is tender, add salt and pepper to taste, stir through once more and serve. I find this dish goes very well with Tortiera di Patate e Funghi (p. 72).

BAKED MACKEREL

SGOMBRO ALLA MARINARA

APULIA

SERVES 4

4 small mackerel or 2 large ones, filleted and heads removed	3 tablespoons capers, chopped
3 tablespoons olive oil	½ chilli pepper, finely chopped
5 tablespoons fresh white breadcrumbs	one 8 oz/227 g can tomatoes, * drained
3 cloves garlic, chopped	20 black or green olives, left whole
12 basil leaves, torn into pieces or ½ teaspoon oregano	juice of ½ lemon

Cut the fish open with sharp scissors and pull out the guts. Wash under running, cold water. Cut off the head with a sharp knife. Open the mackerel out flat and trim the edges carefully. Oil a baking dish large enough to take all the fish in 1 layer. Lay the fish in the dish and sprinkle with a little more oil.

Scatter the breadcrumbs, garlic, capers, basil or oregano, and chilli pepper over the fish. Then chop the tomatoes, put them on top and arrange the olives here and there. Dribble the lemon juice all over the dish, and bake in a lowish oven, gas 3/325°F/160°C, for about 40 minutes. Serve hot as a main course with mashed potatoes and a mixed salad or cold as a starter on their own.

OYSTERS, TARANTO STYLE

OSTRICHE ALLA TARANTINA

APULIA

SERVES 1

6 or 12 oysters	4 tablespoons (approx.) virgin olive oil
plenty of chopped parsley, as fresh as possible	black pepper
4 tablespoons finest fresh white breadcrumbs	

Open the oysters with an oyster knife and throw the empty half shells away. Arrange the oysters on their shells in a large baking dish or on a baking tray.

Scatter with parsley and breadcrumbs, and dribble a little oil over them. Grind some black pepper over the whole dish and place in a medium oven, gas 6/400°F/200°C, for 10 minutes. Serve at once.

UMBRIA

This is the only landlocked region of peninsular Italy, but to make up for its lack of sea coast it has many waterways, and one of the largest lakes in the country – Lake Trasimeno. Its neighbours are Tuscany, the Marche and Lazio and it is an almost entirely hilly or mountainous region where rivers and torrents rush swiftly through the green valleys. The area is famous for the production of sweets and pasta products as well as for steel factories which are situated around the busy central town of Terni.

Apart from its industries, Umbria is mainly rural in its economy, and one of the most important aspects of this is stockraising. Tobacco, olives and grain are also produced here, as is one of the world's most famous Italian wines – the delicious Orvieto.

Norcia is the focal point of Umbrian cuisine as it is here that the black truffle grows profusely and ends up in all manner of local specialities. Stronger in flavour than the white truffle from Alba, this delicious tuber adds spice and style to an otherwise fairly plain and simple rustic cuisine. In the Umbrian kitchen the truffle isn't finely sliced or delicately grated, it is put into the mortar and pounded with a pestle to create divine sauces with anchovies and garlic. It is chopped into chunks and beaten up with eggs to make the world's most memorable omelette. Good simple cooking with few specialities, sums up the food of Umbria. Here you won't find capricious dishes or delicacies prepared with an artist's eye – just plain food that respects the seasons, food that is good for the body as well as the soul.

Biscuits and pastries prepared from ancient recipes and washed down with sweet vin santo finish off most meals – there are hundreds of different kinds of these little cakes, all made with the simplest of local ingredients.

The region is immensely fertile and produces some of the country's best olives. It is known as Green Umbria for its abundance of trees, shrubs and green grass. Medieval towns and villages sit proudly on the hill tops and the beautiful city of Perugia houses a university famous all over the world. Ceramics, cast iron, copper and brass are amongst the region's other commercial benefits.

Look out for the local specialities such as Agnello all'Arrabbiata, very young tender mountain lamb cooked over a fierce heat, basted with olive oil and sprinkled with vinegar. All the marvellous fish that is caught in Lake Trasimeno has a subtly marshy flavour that is typical of fresh water fish; it is fried, boiled or grilled, served just with lemon juice and olive oil – a dish for a king! Fat and juicy pigeons are served in hundreds of different ways – each one better than the last.

In Rome, the word norcino has come to mean pork butcher, so skilled are the people of Norcia in the preparation of pork for hams, sausages and salame. Spaghetti alla norcina is simply spaghetti dressed with masses of black truffles.

Apart from Orvieto, the only other wines I shall mention are the delicious demi-sec Sacrantino, which has a lovely red colour and brilliant flavour; and the amber coloured Greco which has a refreshing though slightly sweetish flavour.

LE MARCHE

In medieval times the region was made up of three areas, each governed feudally by representatives of Rome. They were named Marca di Camerino, Marca di Ancona and Marca di Fano from the ancient German word mark – meaning border or confine. Thus they have been given the collective plural name Marche. Surrounded by five regions and squashed up against the Republic of San Marino, this is a beautiful region of sharp contrasts with craggy mountains that give way to softly rounded hills that slope down to a narrow coastline. Here the deep blue Adriatic laps gently at rocky beaches and important ports like Ancona. Tourists flock to the many seaside resorts on the coast and also to visit the artistic treasures of towns like Urbino. Pilgrims gather frequently at the Santa Casa di Loreto in the province of Ancona.

The region produces little wine due to the general infertility of the soil but one or two are worth mentioning for their superior quality. The most famous is Castello di Jesi Verdicchio which is a lovely dry white wine to serve chilled with fish or as an aperitif. You can't miss it as it always comes in bottles shaped like amphorae. It improves greatly with ageing. Montepulciano Piceno, from the province of Ascoli Piceno, and Rosso Montesanto are two good red wines with a firm body that go very well with roasts of all kinds.

As far as the rest of the local agriculture goes, the infertile soil works against man, limiting the number of crops. Sugar beet is harvested, as are beetroot, fennel, barley and cauliflower. Apart from this poor agricultural commerce, the region counts upon its craftsmen for financial success – the most important local craft being the making of ceramics; those of Urbino are famous all over the world. Tourism brings in the rest of the funds required.

Here, as elsewhere in Italy, we have the contrast between the food that comes from the sea – inspired dishes such as the marvellous Brodetto, a concentrated shellfish soup, flavoured and coloured with saffron and other spices – and the food that comes from the countryside, like the magical Porchetta, a whole roast suckling pig that is turned slowly over an open fire.

If there is one thing which typifies the cuisine of the Marche perfectly it is the way everything is stuffed, smothered in condiment, and drowned in generous sloshes of wine. This is a hearty cuisine, where every dish is cheerfully succulent and rich. Even olives are stuffed and fried and served as a dish in their own right! Prosciutto is never sliced, as in other regions, but always eaten cubed. Fragrant pasties and pies are filled to bursting point with all kinds of fish, free-range chickens are stuffed with olives, and tagliatelle here is made by adding fine white semolina to the dough, which makes the tagliatelle smooth and soft as silk.

5
MEAT DISHES

PORK FILLET WITH CAPERS

FILETTI DI MAIALE CON CAPPERI

UMBRIA

SERVES 4

1 lb/500 g pork fillet,
finely sliced

4 tablespoons olive oil

1 glass dry red wine

juice of ½ lemon

salt and pepper

1 heaped tablespoon
capers

Heat the oil in a frying pan until just smoking and then add the meat. Brown on both sides for 4-5 minutes, then pour in the wine and lemon juice. Simmer gently for 5 minutes then season with salt and plenty of freshly ground black pepper. Scatter the capers over the meat and cook for another 2 minutes to allow some of the liquid to evaporate so that the sauce thickens slightly. Arrange the meat on a platter and pour the sauce over it. Serve as a main course with fresh vegetables.

LAMB STEW

SPEZZATINO DI MONTONE

TRENTINO-ALTO ADIGE

SERVES 4-6

1 onion, chopped

2 cloves garlic, crushed

2 bay leaves, broken into
pieces

large pinch of marjoram

6 tablespoons olive oil

2 lb/1 kg stewing lamb or
mutton, on the bone if
possible

6 medium-sized potatoes,
peeled and cut into
quarters

1 heaped tablespoon
tomato purée*

salt and pepper

Fry the onion, garlic and herbs in the oil until the onion is transparent. Then add the meat, cut into pieces, and raise the heat a little so as to brown and seal it thoroughly on all sides. Pour a ladleful of hot water over the meat, stir and place a lid on the sauce-

pan. Lower the heat and simmer gently for 45 minutes or until the meat is half cooked. Then add another ladleful of water, the tomato purée and season with salt and pepper.

Stir often as the stew continues to simmer, adding more hot water as necessary to prevent sticking. After a further 30 minutes add the potatoes and continue to cook until they have almost fallen apart – they should form a thickish gravy. Stir thoroughly and serve with Radicchio Rosso all'uso Trevisano (p. 73).

BEEF OLIVES WITH GARLIC

COIETAS

SARDINIA

SERVES 4

8 beef olives	ladleful of hot stock
fistful of fresh parsley, chopped finely	salt and pepper
	Sauce
4 cloves garlic, chopped finely	1 onion, finely chopped
2 oz/50 g smoked streaky bacon, chopped finely	6 ripe tomatoes
	salt and pepper
4 tablespoons olive oil	

Cook the ingredients for the sauce together over low heat for 30 minutes.

Meanwhile, flatten out the beef olives as thinly as possible with a mallet. Trim the edges to neaten. Mix together the parsley, garlic and bacon and spread this mixture evenly over each piece of meat. Roll them up and secure each one with 2 toothpicks.

Fry the beef olives on all sides in the olive oil, then add a little stock to keep them moist. When they are cooked through – about 10 minutes – season; sieve the sauce over the meat, and serve.

LAMB WITH OLIVES

AGNELLO ALLE OLIVE

ABRUZZO-MOLISE

SERVES 4

1½ lb/750 g very young lamb, from any tender cut, boned and sliced very thinly	4 oz/125 g black olives, stoned and finely chopped
	pinch of oregano
3 tablespoons plain flour	¼ red chilli pepper, very finely chopped
6 tablespoons olive oil	juice of ½ lemon
salt	

Toss the lamb lightly in flour, then fry it in the olive oil over a high heat. Season with salt and turn the meat over after about 3 minutes. Drain some of the oil out of the pan and lower the heat.

Scatter the olives, chilli and oregano over the meat and stir. Pour over the lemon juice and cook for a further 5 minutes before serving.

Traditionally lamb dishes from this region are served with fried potatoes and cold boiled spinach or Swiss chard tossed in olive oil and vinegar.

STUFFED BEEF ROLL

FARSUMAGRU (FALSOMAGRO)

SICILY

SERVES 6-8

1 very large slice of rump steak, weighing about 1 lb 3 oz/600 g	1 tablespoon chopped parsley
11 oz/350 g ground beef or veal	2 cloves garlic, chopped
7 oz/200 g sausage meat	2 tablespoons fresh white breadcrumbs, soaked in milk
7 oz/200 g Parma ham or other prosciutto crudo,* chopped	½ teaspoon mixed spice
	salt and pepper
1 thick slice smoked back bacon, chopped	3 tablespoons olive oil
	1 onion, very finely sliced
4 oz/125 g pecorino* or Parmesan* cheese, grated or cubed	1 glass dry red wine
	5 tablespoons fresh tomato sauce (p. 74) or puréed tomatoes*
6 eggs	

The name farsumagru means falsely lean as the dish has the appearance of not being a red meat dish at all once it is served with its coating of fresh tomato sauce. The dish is served cold and makes an interesting and original idea for picnics.

Flatten the meat out with a mallet to a thickness of approximately ¼ in/5 mm. To make the filling mix the ground meat, sausage meat, ham, bacon and cheese together in a bowl, then add 1 whole egg and 1 egg yolk, the parsley, garlic, breadcrumbs, spice, salt and pepper.

Mix all to a smooth purée and set aside.

Hard boil the remaining 4 eggs, cool, peel and slice them, discarding the white tips. Spread the filling across the steak and arrange the sliced eggs in the centre. Roll the meat up on itself and tie it up securely with string.

Heat the oil in a casserole and add the onion, fry gently until the onion is lightly coloured, then place the meat roll on top and brown it on all sides. Pour the wine over the meat, then add the tomato sauce. Season and cover. Simmer for 30 minutes, basting occasionally with a little warm water.

You should end up with a good thick sauce. Turn off the heat and leave the meat to cool down in the sauce, then lift it out and slice it thinly. Serve each portion smothered with the sauce and accompany it with Cianfotta (p. 76).

ROAST PORK WITH ROSEMARY

ARISTA ALLA FIORENTINA

TUSCANY

SERVES 6

2 tablespoons fresh rosemary leaves or 1 tablespoon dried rosemary	salt and freshly ground black pepper
	joint of boned pork loin, weighing approx. 3 lb/1.5 kg
2 cloves garlic, finely chopped	

If using fresh rosemary, chop very finely. Whether using the dried or fresh herb, mix the garlic and the rosemary together and season with plenty of salt and fresh black pepper. Make lots of deep holes in the meat with a sharp skewer and fill these with the rosemary, garlic, salt and pepper mixture.

Tie up the joint securely, season generously all over and place in a preheated oven at gas 3/325°F/160°C and allow to roast for about 2 hours, basting occasionally with its own fat and turning it over at each basting. Use a spit if your oven has this facility.

Usually the meat is allowed to cool and served cold the following day but, if you prefer, you can eat it hot like a normal pork roast. Meat cooked in this way keeps very well for several days.

BRAISED BEEF WITH BAROLO

BRASATO AL BAROLO

PIEDMONT

SERVES 6

2 lb/1 kg topside	pinch of grated nutmeg
3 oz/75 g streaky bacon, cut into long thin strips	pinch of mixed spice
2 tablespoons chopped fresh parsley	2 oz/50 g butter
8 leaves fresh sage, chopped finely, or 1 teaspoon dried sage	4 tablespoons olive oil
large sprig of fresh rosemary, chopped finely, or 1 teaspoon dried rosemary	1 small onion, finely sliced
2 cloves garlic, chopped finely	3 tablespoons plain flour
salt and pepper	1 large carrot, sliced thinly
	1 stick celery, sliced thinly
	2 bay leaves
	3 sprigs of fresh parsley, washed and left intact
	1 bottle of Barolo wine

Wrap the strips of bacon around the beef and tie it up securely with string. Place the chopped parsley, sage, rosemary, garlic, salt and pepper, nutmeg and mixed spice in a saucepan and fry together gently in the butter and olive oil for 10 minutes. Add the onion and fry until it is soft and transparent.

Roll the meat in a little flour and then put it in with the other ingredients. Raise the heat and turn the meat in the fried mixture to seal and brown it on all sides. Add the carrot, celery, bay leaves and parsley, and continue to turn the meat over. Remove the meat and skim off any excess grease from the pan. Put in the remaining flour and mix it in carefully. Pour in 1 glass of wine, stir until the mixture is thick and creamy, then return the meat to the saucepan and pour the rest of the wine over it.

Cover with a lid and cook for 4 hours over a low heat. After 4 hours, check to see if the meat is cooked and taste the sauce for seasoning. If necessary, cook longer and adjust seasoning.

Remove the meat, slice thinly and arrange on a warmed platter. Sieve the sauce and pour over the sliced beef before serving.

LIVER AND ONIONS VENETIAN STYLE

FEGATO ALLA VENEZIANA

VENETO

SERVES 4

fistful of parsley, finely chopped	ladleful of hot stock, if necessary
4 tablespoons olive oil	salt and pepper
4 oz/125 g butter	4 slices white bread, crusts removed, cubed and fried in butter
3 onions, finely sliced	
1¼ lb/625 g calves' liver, very finely sliced	

Put the parsley, oil and half the butter into a pan until the butter and oil are hot. Add the onions and fry gently until the onions are soft but not coloured. Set aside. Fry the calves' liver quickly in the remaining butter for about 5 minutes – adding a little stock, if necessary. Season with salt and pepper.

Arrange the onions on a heated dish, lay the slices of cooked liver on top and surround with the hot croûtons. Serve at once with mashed potatoes.

BOLOGNESE MEAT LOAF

POLPETTONE ALLA BOLOGNESE

EMILIA-ROMAGNA

SERVES 6

1 lb/500 g ground beef	rind of ½ lemon, grated finely
3 tablespoons Parmesan, * grated	5 tablespoons milk (more may be required)
large pinch of cinnamon	6 tablespoons sunflower oil
salt and pepper	1 large onion, chopped
4 tablespoons fresh white breadcrumbs	2 tablespoons butter
2 eggs, beaten	
juice of 1 lemon	

Mix the meat with the Parmesan, cinnamon, salt and pepper, half the breadcrumbs, the eggs, the lemon juice and the lemon rind. Add enough milk to make the mixture moist but not sticky.

Fashion the meat mixture into a sausage shape and roll it in the remaining breadcrumbs. Heat the sunflower oil in a large frying pan. Put in the meat and fry quickly on all sides to seal it, then take out and drain thoroughly on kitchen paper.

Fry the onion in butter and put it in the bottom of a baking tin. Lay the polpettone on top and place in a medium oven, gas 5/375°F/190°C. Bake for 30-40 minutes and then serve sliced, hot or cold, with Fresh Tomato Sauce (p. 74).

LIGURIAN VEAL STEW

SPEZZATINO DI VITELLO ALLA LIGURE

LIGURIA

SERVES 4

1½ lb/750 g stewing veal, cut into neat cubes	2 globe artichokes, cleaned and quartered
2 tablespoons olive oil	1 pt/600 ml hot bone or beef stock
2 oz/50 g butter	10 oz/300 g fresh or frozen peas
½ tablespoon beef dripping	2 egg yolks
1 onion, chopped	juice of ½ lemon
fistful of parsley, chopped	salt and pepper
8 small new potatoes, scraped	

Heat the olive oil, butter and dripping in a casserole and brown the meat. As soon as it is browned all over, add the onion and parsley, and season with salt and pepper. Fry gently for 10 minutes. When the onion is browned put in the potatoes, artichokes and enough stock to cover. Add fresh peas and stir. Continue to cook for about 40 minutes, adding more broth if necessary. Add frozen peas 10 minutes before cooking is finished.

When the meat is cooked, beat the egg yolks with the lemon juice and pour over the stew. Stir together quickly to scramble the eggs and then serve.

LAZIO

The region surrounding the nation's capital is a mixture of several different landscapes, some originating from volcanic eruptions in times long past and others green and soft in sharp contrast. The entire region is cut in half by the River Tiber which flows through the city of Rome. The region has a high agricultural production level, probably one of the top three in the country, and this is the most important of its industries.

The Pontine marshes used to be an area where mosquitoes and malaria were the only things available; nowadays, having been drained and restructured, they form an enormous fertile field dotted with houses and farms.

The sea and the mountain chains are Lazio's natural frontiers, in between the Campagna Romana stretches out under the broiling summer sun – an inspiration to many painters and poets throughout the ages. On the volcanic slopes of the Castelli Romani first rate wines are produced under world famous names – even in Roman times, the wines of Tusculum (nowadays known as Frascati) were praised by Horace and Juvenal. These wines are usually white, always mellow and always, whether dry or fruity, delicious and wonderfully thirst quenching on hot summer days. The only other wine I should mention is the famous Est! Est! Est! which is the pride of Montefiascone in the province of Viterbo. This is a harmonious light yellow wine which does much to enhance local cooking.

The cuisine of Lazio deserves more space than I can devote to it here; Rome is one of the most important tourist centres in the world and as such it offers its visitors the gastronomic delights of every large city in the country and abroad. However, there is no local cuisine as such. All the specialities of this region are a combination of things from other regions, because no Roman cook has ever created a culinary masterpiece in the way they have in most other regions. So what you end up with is healthy portions of well seasoned vigorous dishes, typified by the use of garlic, herbs, spices, vinegar and every kind of meat from goat to pork – food that is delicious, though slightly hard on the digestive organs and one's liver.

Excellent cheeses are produced here, the most famous being the piquant pecorino romano made with sheep's milk. The best meat is the superb abbacchio, lamb that has not yet been weaned and has therefore never tasted grass. This is cut into huge chunks and roasted with plenty of oil and herbs and sometimes anchovies. Beef and veal are not special, pork is better and the fat and offal are used very widely. Fish is not common, though eels caught in the Tiber (pollution permitting) are a local speciality. Vegetables are used a great deal, artichokes in particular, and a veritable cornucopia of different kinds of salad.

Rice is used very little, mainly in the preparation of sweets and puddings, and pasta is always heavily dressed with garlic and oil flavoured sauces.

ABRUZZO-MOLISE

Although the two regions of the Abruzzi and the Molise became independent of each other in 1963 they are still generally thought of as one area. It is an area broken up by mountains and hills, from which emerge the massifs of the Gran Sasso, the Maiella, Velino and Mainarda; these lend an imposing and majestic air to the landscape. The green wide valleys around L'Aquila, Sulmona and the Fucino stand out in sharp contrast to the rocky surroundings. The region's economy is based on agriculture and herding although the broken nature of the hilly land makes it almost impossible to grow grain and every bit of level ground has to be used to maximum advantage.

The one-time bed of Lake Fucino, now drained, is one of the most productive areas for growing floury potatoes of excellent flavour. The part of the region that overlooks the Adriatic sea is famous for its garden produce and everywhere in this region one finds sheep – and along with them tasty local cheeses, especially the delicious fresh ricotta. The violent contrast of the landscape is reflected in the eating and drinking habits of the region, together with the extreme poverty of the local resources. The vine struggles for survival on these rocky slopes, producing homely and rather sour wines. The most noticeable feature of the open Molise landscape are the lonely white windmills used to grind flour in the olden days.

The trademark of the cuisine of these parts is the red chilli pepper, scattered with gay abandon over any dish. You may well be offered a plateful of pasta which is red and inviting, and in all innocence will look as though it is dressed with a tomato sauce. One mouthful will have you reeling as the peperoncino sets your mouth on fire. The host will offer you a swig of Centerbe to put the fire out – a liqueur made of more than a hundred mountain herbs which is said to cure anything. The only problem is that as soon as

the Centerbe has put out the fire in your mouth and throat, it lights another in your stomach – filling you with a hot glow from top to toe! This is the essence of the food: malicious, vivacious and spirited. It is almost as though the people of these mountains have created an armour of spices, herbs and chilli against the endless winters, interminable snow falls and icy winds.

Despite its poverty and the small number of local specialities it gives us, it is said that a cook who comes from these parts is an investment for any restaurant. It would appear that nobody can measure out ingredients as accurately as the Abruzzi cook, no other cook can be counted on for such excellent timing and precision as the Abruzzi cook.

One dish which is unique to the region is the delicious hand-made Spaghetti alla Chitarra, pasta rolled out over *la chitarra* (guitar) then pushed firmly through the thin spaces in between the tautly stretched wires. The result is a mass of square spaghetti which get tossed with energy in a sauce of chilli pepper, tomato, smoked bacon and herbs. But not everything is hot and spicy, it is a balanced cuisine where the fiery sauces on pasta are followed by very simply grilled meats and fresh vegetables.

The food prepared along the coast differs considerably from that cooked in the interior. As a general rule, the former has fish as its basis whilst the latter opts for pork. They have the pasta dishes, sweets and vegetable stews in common.

Of the local specialities I shall mention the name that has to win the prize for originality – Polpi in Purgatorio – octopus in purgatory – cooked in parsley, garlic and chilli to create a substantially rich and spicy dish. Scapece is the oldest Abruzzi recipe, consisting of pickled fried fish in white vinegar flavoured with saffron. Parrozzo is the name given to a sweet from the town of Pescara made with almond paste, flour and eggs, with a chocolate coating.

6
POULTRY & GAME DISHES

ROAST PHEASANT

FAGIANO ARROSTO

TUSCANY

SERVES 4

one 3 lb/1.5 kg pheasant	5 fresh sage leaves or
7 oz/200 g prosciutto*	½ teaspoon dried sage
2 oz/50 g streaky bacon	salt and pepper

Wash and wipe the bird carefully. Chop half the prosciutto and add it to the bacon and sage. Chop all 3 ingredients together, then put them inside the pheasant. Wrap it in the remaining prosciutto, season and truss it, then place it in a roasting tin.

Roast in a preheated oven at gas 4/350°F/180°C for about 35 minutes, basting occasionally. Use a little warm water to keep it moist. Remove the bird from the roasting tin and carve it and leave to rest for 10 minutes in a warm place. Pour over the juices from the tin and serve at once with roast potatoes and vegetables.

ROAST PIGEON WITH OLIVES

PICCIONI ALLA PERUGINA

UMBRIA

SERVES 4

4 plump pigeons	2 tablespoons plain flour
4 rashers streaky bacon, chopped	1 glass white wine
4 oz/125 g butter	5 oz/150 g black olives, stoned
1 large onion, sliced thinly	salt and pepper

Place 1 chopped rasher of bacon inside each bird. Season and place them in a casserole with half the butter. Scatter the onion slices over the pigeons, and place the casserole in an oven at gas 3/325°F/160°C. Cook for 30 minutes. Melt the remaining butter in a small saucepan and add the flour, stirring to make a roux. Pour in the wine and mix together thoroughly. Boil to allow the alcohol to evaporate for 3 minutes,

then add the olives and stir together. Remove the birds from the oven, cut in half, pour the olive sauce over them and serve at once.

RABBIT IN A HERB AND TOMATO SAUCE

CONIGLIO ALL'ISCHITANA

CAMPANIA

SERVES 4

3 lb/1.5 kg rabbit portions	1/4 pt/150 ml dry white wine
4 tablespoons olive oil	
6 canned tomatoes, * deseeded and chopped	salt and pepper
	13 fl oz/375 ml boiling water
sprig of rosemary	
7 leaves fresh basil	

Wipe and trim the rabbit, then put in a saucepan and fry it quickly in the oil until browned. Add the tomatoes and herbs, then the white wine. Stir carefully then season. Cook quickly to allow the liquid to reduce somewhat, then pour over the water and put a lid on. The rabbit is ready to be served when all the water has been completely absorbed – this will take about 45 minutes. Serve with a mixed stewed vegetable dish like Piatto d'Erbe alla Lucana (p. 77).

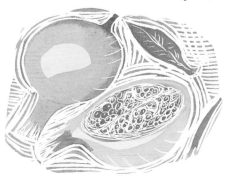

TURKEY WITH POMEGRANATES

PAETA AL MELOGRANO

VENETO

SERVES 6-8

one 6 lb/3 kg turkey, with giblets	5 tablespoons olive oil
	4 dried sage leaves
salt and pepper	3 large ripe sweet pomegranates
3 oz/75 g butter	

Wipe the turkey carefully and reserve the giblets. Rub the bird with salt and pepper both inside and out. Put half the butter inside the turkey and place it in a roasting tin with the rest of the butter, the olive oil and the sage. Roast in a medium oven, gas 3/325°F/160°C for 3 hours, basting frequently. Turn over once during cooking time.

When half cooked (after 1½ hours) pour over the juice of 1 pomegranate. To extract the juice cut the fruit in half and place it upside-down on the juice extractor or lemon juice squeezer. Put a teacup over the fruit – choose one that fits loosely over the fruit – and turn and press down to squash the fruit as much as possible and squeeze out the pink juice.

Chop the giblets very finely and put them in a small saucepan with the juice of the second pomegranate and a little water. Cook gently, stirring to create a smooth sauce. Season with salt and pepper and keep warm until required. While the turkey continues to cook, peel and remove all the red seeds from the third pomegranate. Set them to one side.

When the turkey is tender and cooked through, remove it from the oven and leave it to rest, wrapped in foil, for about 10 minutes. Then carve it and arrange the pieces on a warm platter. Pour the giblet and pomegranate sauce over it, scatter the seeds of the third fruit all over the dish and serve at once.

CHICKEN STUFFED WITH WALNUTS

POLLO RIPIENO ALLE NOCI

TRENTINO-ALTO ADIGE

SERVES 6

one 3 lb/1.5 kg plump chicken, boned if possible	*5 oz/150 g beef bone marrow*
2 stale white bread rolls	*2 oz/50 g chicken livers, chopped*
¼ pt/150 ml milk or chicken stock	*salt and pepper*
2 oz/50 g shelled walnuts, dipped in boiling water, peeled and chopped finely	*2 tablespoons Parmesan,* grated*
2 oz/50 g shelled pine kernels, chopped finely	*1 egg, beaten*
	pinch nutmeg

This dish works perfectly well using a chicken that is not boned but if you wish to be really authentic here's how to bone a chicken. Remove all trussing and place the bird on its back. Holding it with one hand, use the point of a sharp knife to carefully ease out the wishbone. Turn the chicken over and slit the skin all the way down the backbone in as straight a line as possible; you may prefer to use scissors to do this.

Using your fingers, ease the flesh away from the bones on either side of the backbone and down as far as the leg joints. Remove the backbone and ribs. Turn the chicken over and cut the sinews holding the legs to the body. Hold the end of the leg firmly and gradually scrape and push the meat downwards so that the bone pokes out. Do this on both sides and carefully remove the leg bones. Cut off the first joint of the wing and scrape the flesh down, holding the end so as to remove the wing bone in the same way as you did the legs. Do this on both wings. Now very carefully cut the flesh away from the last remaining bone which is the breastbone. Use a very sharp knife and be careful not to pierce it. Reshape the chicken as best you can with your hands.

The most important thing to remember is the order in which the bones are removed: first the wishbone, then the backbone and ribs, then the legs, then the wings and finally the breastbone.

Having boned the chicken you may now make the stuffing. Soak the bread for a few minutes in the milk or stock, then squeeze it well with your hands to remove excess liquid. Mix the chopped nuts together thoroughly. Put the marrow bone into a preheated oven at gas 5/375°F/190°C for 3 minutes, remove it and then slide out the marrow from the bone. Mince or process the marrow with the chicken livers once, then mince again with the bread. Stir in the nuts, salt and pepper, Parmesan, egg and nutmeg.

Fill the chicken with this mixture and sew it up using a large-eyed needle and fine white string. The easiest way to do this is to sew up the neck end first, then fill the chicken from the other end and sew up leaving the tail sticking out. Use large stitches as they will be easier to remove when serving.

Place the chicken in a large boiling pot, cover with water or chicken stock and add a couple of pinches of salt. Bring to the boil, then simmer for 1 hour or until the chicken is tender. Serve hot or cold.

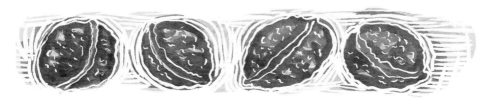

TRUFFLED CHICKEN BREASTS

PETTI DI POLLO TRIFOLATI

LE MARCHE

SERVES 4

1 egg, beaten	2 oz/50 g butter
salt	1 small white truffle, * canned or fresh, chopped finely
4 chicken breasts	
1 tablespoon plain flour (more if required)	5 tablespoons grated Parmesan*
4 tablespoons oil for frying (more if required)	4 tablespoons Cognac
4 thin slices prosciutto crudo*	5 tablespoons single cream

Pour the beaten egg into a soup plate and add a little salt. Toss the chicken breasts in the flour and then coat them with the egg. Fry them in hot oil until golden. Drain and set aside.

Melt the butter in a wide pan then lay in the chicken breasts. Cook them on both sides for about 3 minutes, then put a slice of prosciutto on top of each one. Mix the Parmesan and the truffle together and scatter all over the chicken breasts. Cook under a lid on a low heat for 30 minutes, then pour over the Cognac and the cream.

Remove the chicken breasts and arrange them on a warm platter. Raise the heat to thicken and reduce the sauce in the pan, then pour all over the chicken before serving with peas or spinach.

QUAILS WITH RICE

QUAGLIE AL RISOTTO

LE MARCHE

SERVES 4

8 plump quails	salt and pepper
5 oz/150 g butter	1 glass white wine
4 oz/125 g fatty prosciutto crudo, * chopped finely	2 ladlefuls meat or game stock, kept hot
sprig of fresh thyme or 1/2 teaspoon dried thyme	13 oz/400 g Easy Cook Italian boiling rice
2 bay leaves	6 tablespoons grated Parmesan*

Remove the heads from the quails, then wipe and trim each bird carefully.

Melt half the butter in a casserole with the chopped prosciutto and then lay the quails on top. Add the thyme, bay leaves and seasoning, pour the wine over the birds and cook, covered, for about 30 minutes, basting with the stock from time to time to keep them moist.

When the quails are cooked set them aside and keep warm.

Boil the rice in plenty of salted water. When it is tender, drain it and toss it in a bowl with the remaining butter and the Parmesan.

Arrange the rice on a platter in a crown shape and place the birds on top. Pour the juices from the casserole all over the quails and rice, then serve.

Stuffed Capon

CAPPONE ALLA MANFREDA

EMILIA-ROMAGNA

SERVES 6-8

one 6 lb/3 kg capon or large chicken, boned if possible (see p. 65), otherwise spatchcocked	4 oz/125 g back bacon, chopped
10 oz/300 g minced veal	5 tablespoons Marsala wine
4 oz/125 g prosciutto crudo,* chopped	4 egg whites
4 oz/125 g honey roast ham, chopped	4 hard-boiled egg yolks
	salt and pepper
4 oz/125 g mortadella,* chopped	8 tablespoons olive oil
	2 oz/50 g butter

Wipe and clean the bird and bone it as on p. 65. If you don't want to go to the trouble of boning it, it can simply be split open by cutting through the back. Use a sharp knife to open it up then turn it over and press down hard with the heel of your hand on the breastbone to crack it. Flatten the bird out as much as possible, using your hands to press it. Make a slit where the breastbone has cracked and gently slide it out.

Remove as much fat as possible from the inside of the bird and throw it away or save it for another dish. Also discard the giblets. Mix together the minced veal, prosciutto, ham, mortadella, bacon, Marsala, egg whites and the salt and pepper. Stir to an even texture, then add the sliced hard-boiled egg yolks. Spoon this mixture into the boned or spatchcocked bird and sew it back together again as explained on p. 65. If the bird is not boned you will need to sew it together carefully down the back and the filling will plump out the breast.

Place the capon in a roasting tin and dot with butter. Pour over the oil and roast in a preheated oven gas 4/350°F/180°C. Roast for approximately 2½ hours, basting frequently. Remove the bird from the oven and wrap it in foil. Allow it to rest for 1 hour before carving. Serve warm or cold with a mixed vegetable dish and a mixed salad.

Guinea Fowl with Red Wine

FARAONA AL VINO ROSSO

VENETO

SERVES 4

½ oz/15 g dried mushrooms*	1 tablespoon hot water
1 guinea fowl, cut into 8 pieces	2 tablespoons plain flour
	¼ pt/150 ml dry red wine
7 oz/200 g button onions, chopped finely	2 tablespoons grappa
	salt and pepper
2 oz/50 g butter	pinch of nutmeg
2 oz/50 g streaky bacon, chopped	1 pork sausage with herbs, peeled and chopped

---

Soak the mushrooms in warm water for 20 minutes, then drain, chop and set aside. Wipe and trim the guinea fowl pieces.

Heat half the butter in a saucepan and put in the onions and bacon. Fry gently until browned, then add the water and the guinea fowl. Sprinkle the flour over the guinea fowl and stir carefully to brown the pieces all over. Pour in the wine and grappa. Add the seasoning and nutmeg, stir and cook gently for about 30 minutes.

When the guinea fowl is cooked, remove from the pan and keep warm. Put the sausage, the rest of the butter and the drained and chopped mushrooms in the pan. Stir until the sausage is cooked, then pour the whole lot over the guinea fowl and serve.

CAMPANIA

The coastline of this region dominates half of the landscape with its beauty. The shore line curls round to form gulfs, quiet bays, tiny strips of beach, peninsulas and very steep cliffs, while opposite the islands sit like green jewels in the brilliant blue sea. Vesuvius rises up out of the greenery and it is thanks to the volcano that the land is so fertile, laid out like a chequer board of fields and orchards to grow some of the best fruit and vegetables in the country. It is hard to match the massive amount of produce for the greengrocers that Campania provides for Italy and Europe.

The other face of the region is the rather more lean existence of the people who live in the mountains. Here there is much poverty and communications are very difficult, especially in the winter time when snowfalls make it all the more harsh. Real hardship is still something quite common in certain parts of this region where the constant threat of earthquakes hangs dangerously over everybody's head.

The cuisine of the area revolves around the tomato; cooked very little to retain as much of its brightness as possible, it is then spread over pizza, used to smother spaghetti and fusilli and all other kinds of pasta – a Neapolitan will tell you that with a loaf of bread, tomatoes and olive oil he will survive anything, as long as they come from *his* land!

The wines of the region are all exuberant, refreshing wines that marry so well with the food that they seem to have been created around the local dishes. Biancolella d'Ischia is one of the finest wines produced on the island of Ischia and has a delicate, aromatic bouquet. It's a mellow white wine to be served with delicately flavoured fish dishes. Epomeo is a mellow red wine which ages very well. It goes very well served with roast meat or game or a dish of pasta. Falerno comes in both red and white versions and is made from the special falanghina vines. The red variety was the most famous wine of Roman antiquity – Horace, Pliny, Ovid and Virgil all claimed it to be the proudest and most fiery wine. Capri also comes in a red or white version and both varieties improve as they age. Refreshing, fragrant wines that are the reflection of their place of origin.

The sun seems to shine more brightly in Campania, giving everything you eat warmth and richness. There are no mysteries in the cuisine, what you see spread out in profusion on the market stalls is what you will eat. All kinds of marvellous fish and seafood, delicate, perfumed pastries, baskets brimming with olives, mounds of mozzarella cheeses and cacio cavallo, oranges, prickly pears, melons and tomatoes, more and more tomatoes shining in the sunlight.

Pizza is the centrepiece of the gastronomy. An expertly kneaded dough which is stuffed and folded in half to make calzoni or spread out flat, oiled and covered with tomatoes and seafood, or anchovies, or mushrooms, or prosciutto or whitebait, or garlic and oregano, or basil ... the possibilities are only as limited as the imagination of the cook.

Pasta, pizza, the riches of the sea, superb fruit and vegetables, cheeses and light pastries filled with ricotta and candied fruit, and other imaginative desserts form the basis for the cooking of Campania. Very little meat is cooked here and the most common way of preparing it is, of course, with tomato sauce. An open pan of tomatoes, olive oil, garlic and oregano is left to simmer slowly until you are ready to eat, then the thinly sliced meat is briefly cooked in the sauce and served a la pizzaiola.

Look out for the riches of Fritto Misto, a golden mountain of fried fish, fried ricotta, fried sweetbreads and potatoes and cauliflower. Peppers are split open, stuffed with tomatoes, spices, anchovies and mozzarella, then rolled in breadcrumbs and baked. Zuppa di Mare contains all kinds of sea food and is cooked with tomatoes, garlic, parsley and spices to make a soup that is a meal in itself.

BASILICATA-LUCANIA

This has long been one of the most badly depressed areas of Italy; it is an arid, harsh region, entirely broken up by the Appenines and pre-Appenines so that one can truly say there is not one square metre of plain in the entire area. Only towards the east, where it borders with Apulia and thus meets the Murghe do the slopes become gentler. In recent times, much effort has gone into the improvement of this essentially poverty stricken land. Land reclamation projects are turning the valleys of the Agri and the Sinni into prosperous agricultural areas, and the discovery of oil in the Matera district has given hope to the people of these parts who have always known hardship.

Caesar Augustus made this the third region of Italy, uniting it with Bruttium, which was Calabria. It was named Lucania as it was inhabited by a race called Lucani. Conquered and ruled by Byzantium it became known as Basilicata from the Greek Basilikos, meaning prince or governor. In the 12th century it was taken over by the Normans and the name stuck. The inhabitants are still called Lucani.

So what does this ancient, strange region, where horse-drawn ploughs are still common offer us in the way of food? What can possibly grow here under this incredibly hot sun and amongst the endless stones, especially with such antiquated means of working the stubborn soil?

There is no meat here, or at least, none to speak of. What there is will be lamb, mutton or goat. Without meat, there is almost no soup, because how can you make soup without stock or broth? Pasta therefore comes into its own. If it's home-made, it is hard coarse pasta, made with flour and water and patiently fashioned into a thousand shapes, dressed with the simplest of sauces and eaten hungrily at every meal. There is very little fish, except the trout from the rivers and lakes, and few cheeses. So pasta, lots of pasta, and as a second course, huge portions of vegetables cooked in the oven or fried, flavoured with olives, capers, oregano and chilli. Ginger is used a great deal in these parts, the locals simply call it strong. The Lucani have given Italy one item which is exported all over the world: the delicious Luganega sausage, long and soft and lean. What pork there is will be preserved in many ways – sausages, salame etc.

Basilicata is poor. The food is simple, yet it is perfumed by fresh herbs, stung by peperoncino and garlanded with peppers and aubergines. These are the same flavours that Horace used to tell of and would ask his cook to prepare for him in Rome, so much did he miss this simple, healthy fare.

The wine of this region reflects the climate; it is harsh, robust wine which aims to refresh and cheer. Three are worth remembering: dry red Aglianico del Vulture which is an excellent table wine; the sweet dessert wines called Moscato del Vulture and Malvasia del Vulture – both are white and sparkling. They can be served with desserts.

7
VEGETABLE DISHES

COURGETTES WITH SOUR CHEESE

ZUCCHINE A CASSOLA

SARDINIA

SERVES 4

1 lb 10 oz/800 g courgettes, washed and cubed

1 large onion, sliced

4 tablespoons olive oil

2 tablespoons chopped fresh parsley

6 leaves fresh basil, torn into pieces

1 lb 10 oz/800 g fresh sour white Sardinian cheese, cut into cubes (if unobtainable, use a white cheese with a sour flavour, e.g. Caerphilly)

salt and pepper

Place the vegetables, oil and herbs in a pan and cook together over medium to low heat until the courgettes are soft. Stir often. When the courgettes are cooked, add the cheese and stir together until the cheese is soft and melting. Season the dish and serve very hot.

PEPPERS IN TOMATO SAUCE

PEPERONI ALLA CALABRESE

CALABRIA

SERVES 4

4 large peppers, preferably red and yellow

11 oz/350 g passata* or canned tomatoes,* deseeded and chopped

4 fl oz/125 ml olive oil

2 tablespoons tomato purée*

salt and pepper

Split the peppers and remove the seeds and membranes. Slice into strips, put in a pan and fry them gently in the oil. When the peppers are soft, add the tomatoes and the tomato purée, season and cover with a lid. Cook for 30 minutes, stirring occasionally. Often the peppers are removed from their sauce and used to fill an omelette whilst the remaining sauce is used to dress the pasta for the first course of the meal. If serving the peppers as a vegetable, they can be eaten hot or cold.

MIXED PIEDMONTESE SALAD

GIARDINETTO ALLA PIEMONTESE

PIEDMONT

SERVES 6

10 oz/300 g tiniest new potatoes, washed and scraped

4 bunches radishes, washed and sliced

8 lettuce hearts, (Little Gem) washed and opened out

10 artichoke hearts, preserved in olive oil

juice of 1 lemon, strained

¼ pt/150 ml olive oil

salt and pepper

2 tablespoons chopped parsley

Boil and drain the potatoes and allow to cool. Dress all the vegetables separately with lemon juice, olive oil, salt and pepper and arrange them on a round platter. The name of this dish means little garden and that is how it should look. Begin by putting the lettuce hearts in the centre, leaves spread out and pointing up. Then put the artichoke hearts in a circle around them, and the radishes in a circle around the artichokes with the slices overlapping slightly. Finally arrange the unsliced potatoes around the edge and scatter parsley over them.

This salad is always served with cold meats.

BAKED POTATOES AND MUSHROOMS

TORTIERA DI PATATE E FUNGHI

APULIA

SERVES 6

2 lb/1 kg potatoes, medium-sized

2 lb/1 kg mushrooms, peeled and washed, stalks removed then cap cut in 2 lengthways

3 stale white bread rolls

4 tablespoons chopped fresh parsley

salt and pepper

8 tablespoons pecorino* or Parmesan,* grated

¼ pt/150 ml olive oil

Peel and slice the potatoes and cut them into slices about ½ in/1 cm thick and about the same size as the mushrooms. When buying the ingredients for this dish, try to choose mushrooms that are similar in size to the potatoes.

Process the bread rolls to reduce them to fine crumbs; if you do not own a food processor they can be grated by hand. Mix or process the breadcrumbs, parsley, salt and pepper and grated cheese together.

Oil a large round baking tin or ovenproof dish. Cover the bottom with a layer of potatoes, then cover with half the mushrooms. Scatter over half the breadcrumb mixture evenly, then pour over a little olive oil.

Use the rest of the potatoes to make another layer, then cover with the remaining mushrooms. Cover completely with the reserved breadcrumb mixture, pour over the rest of the oil and place in a medium oven, gas 3/325°F/160°C, for 1 hour before serving as a vegetable with a meat or fish main course or as an accompaniment to an onion or courgette omelette.

Use 6 garlic cloves, chopped finely, and scatter over each layer for a more piquant flavour.

FRIED RADICCHIO

RADICCHIO ROSSO ALL'USO TREVISANO

VENETO

SERVES 6

1 head of radicchio per person, washed and trimmed (the best radicchio is Trevisana)

¼ pt/150 ml olive oil

salt and pepper

Shake out all the water from each head of radicchio and then cut them in half or in quarters, according to their size. Dress them thoroughly in a bowl as though you were making a salad, with the olive oil and the salt and pepper.

Heat a cast-iron pan and fry the radicchio in oil for 5 minutes on each side. If a lid is placed on the pan they will become soft and delicately flavoured; if cooked uncovered they will remain crisper and slightly more bitter. Serve as soon as they are cooked through.

This dish is often served as a starter on its own but also goes very well with steaks or any red meat dish, especially if barbecued.

AUBERGINES IN TOMATO AND ONION SAUCE

MELANZANE ALLA PARMIGIANA

EMILIA-ROMAGNA

SERVES 4

4 medium-sized aubergines, sliced lengthways

1 large onion, sliced

6 tablespoons olive oil

½ oz/15 g butter

3 oz/75 g prosciutto crudo, * chopped

8 canned tomatoes, * deseeded and chopped

salt and pepper

Boil the sliced aubergines in salted water for 5-10 minutes or until tender. Drain and lay out on a tea cloth in a warm place to dry out completely – preferably in the hot sunshine.

Heat the oil and butter in a saucepan and fry the onion and prosciutto. When the onion is transparent, add the tomatoes and cook gently. Season and simmer for about 20 minutes, then add the aubergines, cover with a lid and simmer even more slowly for 1 hour. Serve hot or cold.

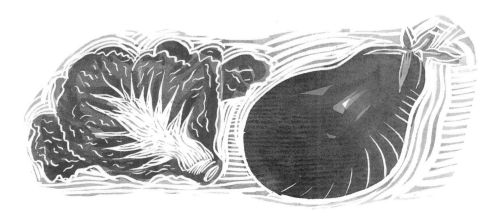

Neapolitan Fresh Tomato Sauce

SALSA DI POMODORO

CAMPANIA

MAKES 1¾ PT/1 LITRE APPROX.

2 lb/1 kg fresh ripe tomatoes	fistful of parsley, left whole
10 leaves basil, torn into pieces	salt
	1 onion, chopped

When the tomato was first introduced into Italy, it was regarded with much suspicion by all and sundry. Many claimed it was a deadly poisonous fruit. It was a Neapolitan cook who first plucked up enough courage to try it out, with the result that tomatoes have become the absolute hallmark of Neapolitan cuisine. In Naples the tomato is always cooked quickly and lightly to preserve as much of its brightness as possible. Here is the traditional tomato sauce which can be kept in the refrigerator and used to enliven any dish in which tomatoes are called for.

Wash and quarter the tomatoes and place in a saucepan with the other ingredients. Cook gently for 30 minutes, then sieve carefully. Pour into a bottle and keep in the refrigerator. Use as required. It will keep for up to a week.

To make it last longer, don't fill the bottle right to the top, but leave room to cover the surface of the sauce with olive oil.

Baked Aubergines with Tomatoes, Cheese and Hard-Boiled Eggs

MELANZANE ALLA PARTENOPEA

CAMPANIA

SERVES 4

4 small aubergines	8 tablespoons (approx.) fresh tomato sauce (see previous recipe)
salt	
oil for deep frying	
7 oz/200 g mozzarella*	1 egg, beaten
4 eggs, hard-boiled	5 tablespoons grated Parmesan*

Cut the aubergines lengthways into fairly thick slices and sprinkle with salt. Place in a colander under a plate and a weight to drain away their bitter juices. After about 1 hour, remove and wash them, pat dry and fry to a golden colour. Drain on kitchen paper and set to one side.

Slice the mozzarella very thinly, then slice the hard-boiled eggs. Oil an ovenproof dish big enough for all the ingredients and cover the bottom with half the tomato sauce. Put in slices of fried aubergine, then slices of mozzarella tossed in the beaten egg, then slices of hard-boiled egg. Cover with the remaining tomato sauce and Parmesan and then repeat the entire layering process. Place in a hot oven, preheated to gas 6/400°F/200°C, and bake for 15 minutes before serving.

COLD DEEP-FRIED CAULIFLOWER FLORETS

CAVOLFIORE IN VASTEDDA

SICILY

SERVES 4

1 ½ lb/750 g cauliflower, divided into florets	*3 eggs, beaten*
8 oz/250 g plain flour	*salt and pepper*
3 canned or salted anchovies, boned, washed and dried, then chopped finely	*olive oil (enough to deep fry the cauliflower)*

Boil the cauliflower for 6-7 minutes in salted water. Meanwhile stir cold water into the flour with a fork. Mix and add more water until you have a paste that is smooth and has the texture of thick cream. Stir the anchovies into this mixture. Beat salt and pepper into the beaten eggs.

Heat the oil until sizzling. Drain the cauliflower carefully and dip each floret into the flour mixture, then into the egg and then into the oil to fry to a golden brown. Drain and sprinkle with a little salt before leaving to cool.

Traditionally this dish is served cold, but personally I like it hot and serve it as a starter with anchovy sauce (see next recipe).

ANCHOVY SAUCE

SALSINA D'ALICI

LAZIO

SERVES 2-4

4 canned or salted anchovies, washed and bones removed	*2 tablespoons olive oil*
2 cloves garlic, chopped	*9 tablespoons milk*
	pepper

Put the anchovies, garlic and oil into a small saucepan over medium heat. As the oil gets hotter, mash the anchovies with a fork and mix them with the garlic. When you have a smooth paste add the milk and mix together until creamy. Season with pepper before serving.

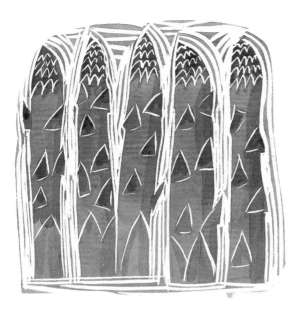

COLD MIXED VEGETABLE STEW

CIANFOTTA

CAMPANIA

SERVES 4

2 aubergines, cut in 2 in/5 cm cubes	1 stick celery, chopped thinly
10 oz/300 g fresh ripe tomatoes, peeled	10 tablespoons olive oil
1½ lb/750 g potatoes, peeled	2 courgettes, cubed
1 lb/500 g onions, sliced	1½ lb/750 g sweet yellow peppers
8 leaves fresh basil, torn up	salt and pepper

Put the aubergines into a colander and sprinkle with salt. Put a plate on top of the aubergines, place a book or heavy weight on top of the plate and put the colander in the sink for 1 hour to allow the bitter juices to drain out. Sieve the tomatoes and set aside. Cut the peeled potatoes into cubes.

Put the onions, basil and celery into a casserole and fry gently in the oil until the onions have become soft. Add the tomatoes and stir together thoroughly. As soon as the mixture begins to bubble, add the potatoes, rinse and dry the aubergines and put them in; and finally the courgettes. Stir and cook very, very slowly, adding a little water from time to time to keep it moist. Split and deseed the peppers and cut them into neat strips. Add them to the other vegetables after 20 minutes. When all the vegetables are cooked through but not mushy, remove from the heat and cool completely before serving.

VARIATION

Cianfotta makes a delicious filling for vegetarian lasagne especially if you alternate green and yellow layers of pasta.

ASPARAGUS WITH PARMESAN CHEESE

ASPARAGI ALLA PARMIGIANA

EMILIA-ROMAGNA

SERVES 4

2½ lb/1.25 kg asparagus	salt
4oz/125 g Parmesan, * grated	4 oz/125 g butter, melted

Scrape and wash the asparagus and tie them up in bundles. Boil them in a large pan in salted water for just 9 minutes, then drain carefully and arrange them in an ovenproof dish. Pour the butter all over them, cover with the Parmesan and place in a hot oven, gas 5/375°F/190°C, for 5-10 minutes before serving as a starter or vegetable dish.

Mixed Vegetable Casserole

PIATTO D'ERBE ALLA LUCANA

BASILICATA-LUCANIA

SERVES 6

2 large aubergines, cut into 2 in/5 cm cubes

3 very large onions, cut into thin rings

¼ pt/150 ml olive oil

2 large yellow peppers, sliced into strips

2 extra large ripe tomatoes, peeled and deseeded, then chopped

fistful of fresh basil, chopped

fistful of fresh parsley, chopped

4 cloves garlic, chopped finely

salt and pepper

Put the aubergines in a colander, sprinkle with salt and leave under a plate with a weight on top to allow all the bitter juice to drain out. After 30 minutes wash the aubergines and pat them dry. Fry the onion rings in the oil until soft, then add the aubergines and mix together. Add the peppers and tomatoes and stir; cook gently for 10 minutes. Then add the basil, parsley, garlic and seasoning. Cook without a lid over a low heat for 40 minutes or until soft and cooked right through.

I find this dish goes down well as a starter with garlic toast which I make by toasting thickish slices of crusty bread under the grill. Then one side is rubbed with a clove of garlic and the bread is laid out on a platter. I pour olive oil over each slice of bread (about ½ tablespoon per slice) and a light sprinkling of salt and pepper finishes it off.

Broad Beans with Ham

FAVE AL PROSCIUTTO

TUSCANY

SERVES 4

4 lb/2 kg broad beans in their pods

1 onion, chopped

fistful of fresh parsley, chopped

13 oz/400 g prosciutto crudo,* chopped

6 tablespoons olive oil

¼ pt/150 ml dry white wine, preferably Tuscan

salt and pepper

Shell the broad beans and soak them in cold water until required. This will remove any bitterness and will improve their texture. Fry the onion, parsley and prosciutto in a terracotta or cast iron casserole with the oil. When the onion is soft add the beans and stir together. Cover and cook for 20 minutes, then pour over the wine and season to taste. Simmer slowly and stir occasionally until the beans are soft. Serve hot as an accompaniment to game dishes such as roast pheasant.

APULIA

The landscape of this region is the most flat of all the regions of Italy. Here there are no Appenine mountains to break up the land; just one mountain range rises up on the border with neighbouring Molise. It is a narrow region with a very long coastline which forms the heel of Italy's boot. From the sleepy, hot port of Brindisi, ships set sail regularly for the Greek port of Patras and it is nearby Greece that has always had an influence on the people and the traditions of Apulia.

From Greece, Apulia has stolen its colours, flavours and style. The food is the food of simple shepherds who like things to be uncomplicated, wholesome and full of goodness. It is common in these parts to find the meals limited to a single dish; for example, Lanache di Casa are wide home-made tagliatelle that are layered with stuffed mussels so as to make one single appetising and filling course, or pasta dressed with stuffed peppers or aubergines, or delicious pies filled with vegetables and cheese.

Apulia is a part of Italy that even Italians don't know very well. Life in the deep south is slow and traditional, with saints' days and village ceremonies marking time, each festivity punctuated by the preparation of the traditional dishes to mark the day, as they have done for centuries.

The dishes are perfumed with bay leaves and other herbs, the cakes and puddings flavoured with honey, and the olive gets in everywhere. Lamb is the meat most used, cooked in many varied ways, always succulent and tasty. When I think of the cooking of Apulia I think of Orecchiette, those neat 'little ears'

– pasta made with flour and water and the addition of fine semolina, which is shaped into round, concave ear shapes by rolling them over a rough table top with the thumb. They are served with lamb chops in a tomato sauce, or with turnip tops and olive oil to make one of the most famous local specialities, or potatoes to make a superb dish flavoured with rue.

But with such a long coastline, we must not forget the fish. Top of the list are the juicy oysters from Taranto, then the mussels, squid, sardines, whitebait and mullet. All fish is cooked simply yet imaginatively, retaining all the freshness and flavour of the sea.

The fruit of the area deserves a special mention; there are incredibly juicy, sweet figs, yellow melons which must be chilled before eating, cooling pink watermelons and delicious grapes.

To complement this simple, tasty cuisine are excellent local wines. The red and white versions of Castel del Monte are good very dry wines that will cheer and refresh you. The rosé version is superb and should be saved for special meals. Barletta is a dark garnet red wine from the area of Troia and is so full-bodied and alcoholic as to be often used in the improvement of other wines. There are many dessert wines to be found in the area, Moscato delle Murge is one that goes particularly well with almond paste confectionery. Mistella is a reddish orange dessert wine with a very rounded, fleshy flavour. Moscato di Trani and Moscato di Salento are two white dessert wines with a warm, velvety flavour.

CALABRIA

Calabria is a land of strength and silence, of mystery and poverty and old customs. The people here are decisive and strong; the men leave their families for months on end to travel north, some even as far as Germany, to seek work, leaving their women and children at home to cope alone. This region is poor, it uses what it has to keep itself going, and is an easy target for its own version of the Mafia, which in these parts is called 'l'Andrangedda'. Calabrian men are tough, dark and insanely jealous, filling the national newspapers with tales of their latest crime of passion. The woman's place is quite definitely in the kitchen, producing some of the best of Italy's food, and in the bedroom producing more and more children.

The landscape is austere, dominated by the huge Sila mountain with its many artificial lakes and vast forest, and embraced by the blue sea on three sides. The region's capital is Reggio Calabria and although three quarters of the region is covered by mountains, what little flat land is left is fertile and well cultivated. Citrus fruits, olives and vines grow well and form an important part of the local economy, supplemented by an ever increasing tourist trade.

A holiday in Calabria means you will find remote, isolated and empty beaches with soft clean sand to sunbathe on in scorching heat; but in contrast you can take long rambling walks up in the mountains where the temperatures are definitely cooler.

As far as food goes, the pig is king. Allowed to trundle freely through the streets surrounded by its offspring and cared for by all and sundry, it meets its end in the autumn, when it is ceremoniously slaughtered. The occasion is marked with a great party held around an open fire and all the best parts of the animal are eaten by the participants. Once the singing is over, the family gets down to business putting the rest of the pork away for the winter; you have to live here to know just how hard the winter months can be. All manner of delicious sausages, salame and ham are created out of the meat and the offal, and put away for cold winter days.

As so much of the region is mountainous, it is quite naturally the mountain cooking which dominates the gastronomical scene. The marvellous mountain cheeses will be eaten at any hour of the day, with a hunk of bread and a glass of wine; best known are Buttirro, Rinusu, Tuma, Impanata and Caciocavallo. Huge red-capped mountain mushrooms also form part of the local cuisine, along with the sour-tasting wild onion called 'cipudizza', and the fat trout that swim in the ice cold lakes.

Much of Calabrian cooking is plain, unfussy, unimaginative and has about it a rather strict, old fashioned quality. But you cannot say the same about their pasta making, nor about their fantastic selection of cakes and pastries. The pasta comes in a thousand different shapes, all hand-made with great patience by women, shrouded in black, bent over their tables. The pasta will be generously dressed with fragrant sauces, or layered with meat and mozzarella to make a very filling lasagna. Pastries and cakes remind one of the Arab markets whence they originated. Gooey, sweet and sticky, they come in many colours and shapes and are often fried in hot oil, filling the houses with the scent of aniseed, liqueurs of all kinds, honey, almonds and mountains of sugar.

As far as the wines go, the most noteworthy are the soft Melissa and Melitino, both white, and the harsher dry reds, Savuto and Pollino, that marry perfectly with roasted meats, sausages and cheese.

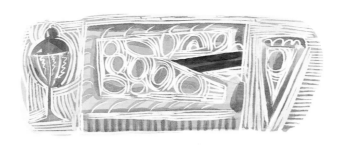

8
CAKES AND DESSERTS

STRAWBERRY CAKE

TORTA DI FRAGOLE

TRENTINO-ALTO ADIGE

SERVES 6

10 oz/300 g strawberries (the original recipe calls for wild woodland berries)

6 tablespoons Kirsch or strawberry aqua-vitae or eau-de-vie

2 tablespoons granulated sugar

¼ pt/150 ml whipped cream, sweetened with 1 tablespoon sugar

10 oz/300g round sponge cake, about 8 in/20 cm in diameter

10 whole strawberries

3 tablespoons icing sugar, sifted

Cut up the hulled strawberries and soak them for 1 hour in the Kirsch, granulated sugar and 3 tablespoons water. Chill the whipped cream. Spread the strawberries all over the sponge cake and cover with the cream. Decorate with the whole strawberries, dust with icing sugar and chill until required.

ZABAIONE

ZABAIONE

PIEDMONT

SERVES 4

4 egg yolks

4 tablespoons dry Marsala or white wine with a strong flavour

4 tablespoons sugar

4 tablespoons cold water

Put all the ingredients in a saucepan capable of taking twice the volume, with a comfortable handle and of an easy weight. If you have a copper sugar boiler that is the best pan to use. Whisk everything together very thoroughly. Stand the pan in a larger saucepan containing hot water and place it all on a medium heat. Proceed to whisk the egg mixture evenly and rhythmically without stopping or changing direction. Whisk for about 18 minutes by which time the zabaione will have doubled in volume and will be fluffy and pale yellow. The zabaione must not

boil; you do *not* want something which has the consistency of scrambled egg, so remove from the heat from time to time and whisk on a work surface instead. If you want to, you can use an electric hand whisk, but the bowl or pan containing the zabaione must still be held over hot water.

As soon as it is as light and fluffy as a soufflé, pour it into 4 tall glasses and serve at once, or allow to cool, refrigerate and serve very cold.

STUFFED PEACHES

PESCHE RIPIENE

PIEDMONT

SERVES 6

6 large firm ripe yellow peaches or 12 small ones	1 tablespoon cocoa powder
10 peeled almonds, chopped finely	3 oz/75 g butter
3 oz/75 g amaretti or ratafia biscuits, crumbled	1 glass Moscato or other dessert wine
2 oz/50 g granulated sugar	

Cut the peaches in half with care and remove the stones. Scoop a little of the peach away from the centre of each one and put the pulp in a bowl. Mix together the chopped almonds and the crumbled biscuits, and add the scooped-out peach flesh. Put in the sugar, except for 2 tablespoons, and the cocoa. Mix very thoroughly and then use this mixture to fill each half peach.

Butter a baking dish and arrange the half peaches in it. Dot them with the remaining butter, pour over the wine and dust with the rest of the sugar. Bake in a hottish oven, gas 6/400°F/200°C, for 40 minutes. Serve hot with very cold whipped cream or a good, rich Italian vanilla ice-cream.

CHESTNUT CAKE

TORTA DI CASTAGNE

FRIULI-VENEZIA GIULIA

SERVES 6

13 oz/400 g fresh chestnuts	4 oz/125 g butter, softened and cut into pieces
4 oz/125 g peeled almonds, chopped	grated rind of 1 lemon
4 eggs, separated	7 oz/200 g whipped cream, sweetened to taste and chilled
7 oz/200 g sugar	

Pierce the chestnuts with a fork, put them into a pan, cover with water and boil until soft. Drain and remove the shell and the inner brown skin. Peel and mash the chestnuts finely whilst still hot, mix the almonds and the chestnut purée together. Beat the egg yolks until pale yellow, add the sugar, all but 2 tablespoons of butter, the lemon rind and the chestnut and almond mixture. Beat this together very thoroughly until you have a smooth light texture. Whisk the egg whites until stiff then fold them in carefully. Butter and flour a round cake tin 8 in/20 cm in diameter and pour the mixture into it. Bake in a moderate oven, gas 4/350°F/180°C, for 35 minutes. Cool on a wire tray in the tin, turn out onto a platter and serve with the whipped cream.

Note: canned unsweetened purée can be used, but the flavour will not be the same. However it does save a lot of time and burnt fingers as chestnuts must be peeled while very hot.

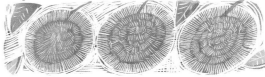

STUFFED PASTRY ROLL

GUBANA

FRIULI-VENEZIA GIULIA

SERVES 6

11 oz/350 g plain flour	rind of ½ lemon, grated
10 oz/300 g butter	rind of ½ orange, grated
1 egg	1 tablespoon fresh
4 tablespoons grappa	breadcrumbs
3 oz/75 g sultanas,	2 oz/50 g butter
soaked for 15 minutes in	1 egg, separated
a little sweet wine	1½ oz/40 g almonds,
4 oz/125 g shelled	blanched and chopped
walnuts, chopped finely	2 tablespoons melted
3 oz/75 g pine kernels	butter
1½ oz/40 g candied	1 egg, beaten
orange peel, chopped	2 tablespoons granulated
1½ oz/40 g candied lime	sugar
peel, chopped	

Take one third of the flour and the butter and rub them together or process to make a rich shortcrust pastry. When you have made a smooth ball of pastry dough set it aside under a clean tea cloth until required. Mix together, using your hands or the food processor again, the rest of the flour with the egg and half the grappa. Roll this mixture into a ball of pastry and place it to one side.

Flour your work top and roll out the shortcrust pastry as thinly as possible. Cut it into 3 or 4 oblong pieces of the same size and set them to one side, carefully floured so that they don't stick to each other or the work top. Roll out the second type of pastry in the same way and cut that into 3 or 4 oblong pieces also.

Beginning with a sheet of shortcrust pastry, lay the sheets one on top of the other, alternating between shortcrust and the other kind of pastry. Give each added layer a quick roll of your rolling pin before adding the next layer. Don't squash down hard as you must have a little air space between each layer. However, the final sheet of layered pastry should be longer than what you started with.

Mix together the drained sultanas, walnuts, pine kernels, candied orange and lime peel and the grated lemon and orange rind. Fry the breadcrumbs lightly in the butter then add them to the mixture. Bind together with the egg yolk and mix in the almonds. Give it a really good stir, pouring the rest of grappa in as you mix. Whisk the egg white until really stiff, then fold in.

Spread this mixture out on the pastry very carefully keeping about 2 in/5 cm in from the edges. Start at one end first and spoon on just a little of the filling, then fold the pastry over on itself to cover just that portion of filling. Add another bit of filling and fold the pastry over to cover it. Continue in this way, working along the sheet of pastry which should be longer than it is wide in order to achieve the effect. What actually happens is that the cake comes out like a rough spiral with the filling twisted up inside the folded over pastry casing.

Brush a baking tray with a little melted butter and gently lay the gubana on it. Brush with beaten egg and sprinkle with sugar. Bake in a preheated oven at gas 5/375°F/190°C for 45 minutes. Serve hot or cold with a chilled dessert wine and cold single cream.

CHOCOLATE CAKE

DOLCE TORINO/TORTA GIANDUIA

PIEDMONT

SERVES 8

2 oz/50 g hazelnuts

10 oz/300 g granulated sugar

8 oz/250 g plain chocolate

6 eggs

3 egg yolks

½ teaspoon honey

4 oz/125 g butter

3½ oz/100 g plain flour, sieved

3½ oz/100 g potato starch

1 teaspoon vanilla extract

6 tablespoons double cream

1 tablespoon apricot jam

7 oz/200 g plain chocolate cake covering

3 tablespoons maraschino liqueur

2 tablespoons brandy

butter for greasing and flour for dusting the cake tin

This is rather a lengthy and complicated chocolate and hazelnut cake which is well worth all the trouble it takes to make! The strong liqueur flavour makes it not so suitable for children, but this traditional speciality of the Piedmont region is the ultimate dinner party chocolate dessert.

Toast the hazelnuts in the oven and remove the outer skin. Melt 1 tablespoon sugar in a small saucepan and add the toasted hazelnuts to it. Process or pound this combination to a smooth hazelnut paste.

Melt 3 oz/75 g of the chocolate and set aside. Whisk the 6 eggs, 3 egg yolks and 8 oz/250 g of the sugar together until foamy and thick. Do this with the bowl standing over a saucepan full of warm water; don't allow the water to get any more than hand hot or the cake will be spoiled. Add the honey, remove from the heat and continue to beat until completely cool and thickened.

Place the butter, melted chocolate, vanilla and hazelnut paste in another bowl over a pan full of hot water or in the top of a double boiler and stir until smoothly mixed together.

Sift the flour and potato starch into the egg, sugar and honey mixture and fold in very carefully and gently. Then fold in the butter, chocolate, vanilla and hazelnut mixture. Pour this mixture into a buttered and floured 9 in/22 cm cake tin and place in a preheated oven, gas 5/375°F/190°C, where it must bake for approximately 50 minutes. When the cake is cooked, lift it out of the oven and turn it out onto a clean napkin where it can be left to cool.

Put the rest of the chocolate in a bowl over a pan of hot water or in the top of a double boiler, add the cream and stir to a smooth cream. As soon as it begins to boil, remove from the heat and pour into a bowl to cool, stirring occasionally to prevent a skin forming on the top.

Put the apricot jam in a small saucepan and add 1 tablespoon of sugar. Stir over a low heat until melted, then keep aside in a warm place.

Melt the chocolate cake covering and also keep aside in a warm place. Whip the cream and chocolate mixture until stiff.

Place the cooled cake on a serving platter with a sheet of greaseproof paper underneath it. Slice off the hard crust and cut the cake in half horizontally. Mix the maraschino with the brandy and paint half of it all over the bottom half of the cake. Spread three quarters of the chocolate cream over the bottom half of the cake, then put the other half of the cake on top.

Paint the top of the cake with the remaining liqueur and then coat the cake completely with apricot jam. Spread with the chocolate covering and decorate with the remaining chocolate cream. Remove the greaseproof paper before serving. Do not put it in the refrigerator, but keep it in a cool place until ready to serve.

This cake is traditionally baked in a round tin and has Gianduia written across it with melted chocolate.

STRUDEL FILLED WITH CUSTARD

STRUDEL CON LA CREMA

TRENTINO-ALTO ADIGE

SERVES 6

11 oz/350 g plain flour

2 oz/50 g butter, cut into small cubes

½ tablespoon sugar

1 egg

pinch of salt

2 oz/50 g butter, melted

3 tablespoons fresh white breadcrumbs

large pinch of cinnamon

2 oz/50 g sultanas, soaked for 15 minutes in warm water, drained and dried with care

4 oz/125 g granulated sugar

4 oz/125 g butter, whisked to a soft cream

5 eggs, separated

7 fl oz/200 ml sour cream

¾ oz/20 g plain morning coffee biscuits, pounded to a powder

grated rind of 1 lemon

4 tablespoons icing sugar, sifted carefully

Pour the flour out onto the work surface and make a hollow in the centre. Put the cubed butter, ½ tablespoon sugar, egg and salt into the hollow and knead it in with your hands. Continue to knead until you have a smooth dough, adding as much tepid water as you need. Work it energetically for 5 minutes, then slap it hard against the work surface over and over again for 10-15 minutes to make a really elastic dough.

Roll the dough into a ball and place it in a bowl under a tea cloth in a warm, draught-free position. After about 1 hour, take the dough out of the bowl. Spread a big tablecloth out and roll the dough out on it, flouring the cloth, your hands and the rolling pin first. The dough should make an elongated circle of pastry no thicker than ¼ in/5 mm.

Brush the pastry all over with half the melted butter. Scatter the breadcrumbs over the surface and sprinkle with the cinnamon, sultanas and about 2 oz/50 g of sugar.

In a bowl, whisk the softened butter and the remaining sugar. Then add the 5 egg yolks, one at a time. Be sure that each one has been completely absorbed before adding another. Put in the sour cream, a little at a time. Whisk the egg whites until completely dry and stiff, and fold them, a little at a time, into the mixture with the biscuits and lemon rind. This is a very slow and deliberate procedure – be careful!

Pour this 'custard' onto the sheet of pastry, avoiding the edges. Level it out with a spatula and then roll the pastry over to enclose the filling, using the tablecloth to help you – do not touch the strudel with your hands while you roll it up. Pinch the 2 ends together with your finger and thumb, then gently drop the strudel onto a buttered baking tray without touching it – use the tablecloth again. Brush all over with the remaining melted butter and bake in a moderate oven, gas 4/350°F/180°C, for about 1 hour.

When it is baked, slide onto a cooling grid and dust with icing sugar. Serve warm or cold.

CHOCOLATE AND CREAM DESSERT

ZUCCOTTO

TUSCANY

SERVES 8

For the sponge cake

6 egg yolks

5 oz/150 g icing sugar, sieved

1 teaspoon clear honey

1 teaspoon vanilla extract

6 egg whites

3 oz/75 g plain flour, sieved

3 oz/75 g potato starch, sieved

butter for greasing and flour for dusting the cake tin

For the filling

3 oz/75 g toasted peeled almonds, chopped

3 oz/75 g toasted peeled hazelnuts, chopped

5 oz/150 g dark chocolate, chopped

1¾ pt/1 litre whipping cream, whipped

5 oz/150 g dark chocolate, melted into a smooth cream

5 oz/150 g icing sugar, sieved

3 tablespoons rum

3 tablespoons brandy

3 tablespoons cherry brandy

2 tablespoons cocoa powder, sieved

Beat energetically with a whisk until foamy and pale yellow. Beat the egg whites until stiff and fold into the egg yolk mixture. Then very carefully sift in the flour and potato starch and fold into the mixture very delicately.

Pour this into the cake tin and place in a preheated oven at gas 5/375°F/190°C. Allow to bake for 40 minutes then remove from the oven and ease out of the tin onto a cooling grid. Leave to one side until required.

Now prepare the filling for the zuccotto. Mix the almonds, hazelnuts and chopped chocolate into the whipped cream. Divide it in half and add the melted chocolate to one half of the cream. Sweeten each half of the cream with 2 oz/50 g of icing sugar and stir carefully. Chill until required.

When the cake is cool, slice the crust off the top and cut the cake in half horizontally. Put one half away to use for another time. Cut a circle of lightly oiled greaseproof paper to fit the bowl you will use as a mould and line it. Push the half cake into the bowl and ease it to fit round the sides.

Mix the rum, brandy and cherry brandy together and paint the cake with this mixture so as to soak it completely and help it to firmly fit the mould. Trim off any untidy edges and use your hands to get as smooth a finish as possible. Now spoon the white

This traditional Tuscan dessert is easily recognized by the pattern of icing sugar and cocoa with which it is always decorated. It calls for Italian sponge cake which is called Pan di Spagna.

For the cake you will need a tin with a diameter of approximately 10 in/25 cm. A slightly less wide bowl with smooth sides will serve as a mould for the zuccotto itself.

First make the sponge cake. Butter and flour the cake tin and set it to one side. Put the egg yolks in a bowl with the icing sugar, honey and vanilla extract.

NEAPOLITAN TRIFLE

ZUPPA INGLESE ALLA NAPOLETANA

CAMPANIA

SERVES 12

10 oz/300 g sponge cake, cut into thin strips about 2 in/5 cm wide

10 tablespoons of your favourite liqueur

10 tablespoons dark rum

1 lb 2 oz/550 g fresh ricotta*

4 oz/125 g dark cooking chocolate

5 oz/150 g granulated sugar

2 teaspoons vanilla extract

---

cream mixture on top and smooth it evenly up to the edges. The white cream should dip down towards the middle. Fill the cake and bowl right up to the top with the chocolate mixture and smooth it with a spatula.

Place in a very cold refrigerator for 2 hours or a freezer for 1 hour and then into the fridge for 1 hour.

Cut a circle out of greaseproof paper to approximately the same size as the zuccotto when turned out. Draw on it 8 slices and cut out each alternate slice. When the 2 hours are up, remove the zuccotto from the fridge and turn it out onto a serving platter. Place the paper cut-out over the zuccotto and liberally sprinkle it with the cocoa mixed with all the remaining icing sugar. Then very carefully remove the paper and you will have adorned the zuccotto with its classical design. Keep in the fridge until you serve it.

Arrange a layer of cake strips in the bottom of an attractive bowl. Measure out the liqueur and the rum in 2 separate bowls. Sieve the ricotta into the bowl containing the liqueur, and mix them together. Grate the chocolate and mix 2 tablespoons of it into the ricotta mixture.

Put the sugar and the vanilla in a saucepan over a medium heat with 2 tablespoons of water and stir continuously until you have a foaming, smooth caramel.

Whisk in the ricotta mixture, a little at a time, stirring to create a smooth creamy texture.

Soak the cake in the bowl with a little rum, then cover with a layer of ricotta mixture. Cover with more cake and soak it with rum again.

Spread another layer of ricotta mixture over the cake and continue in this way until you have used up all the ingredients except the chocolate. Scatter the grated chocolate all over the surface of the trifle and place the bowl in the refrigerator for 1 hour before serving.

This bears very little resemblance to an English trifle but it is a delicious alternative. If ricotta is hard to find use ordinary cream cheese.

SICILY

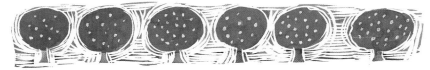

Just 140 km. from the Tunisian coast and with the mere 3 km. width of the straits of Messina separating it from Italy, Sicily lies opposite southern Italy, the largest island in the Mediterranean, and one of the most mysterious. The northern part of the island is industrial and fertile, with considerable fishing activity in its numerous ports and the cultivation of citrus fruits, vines and vegetables occupying the lower mountain slopes.

The western end of the island is also prosperous; it has fertile soil, rich vegetation and excellent vineyards. Trapani is not only a fishing port but a wine making town and salt production centre. The Ionian coast gets its income by means of the well developed tourist trade, the fishing of tuna and swordfish and its agriculture.

The magic of Sicily will ensnare you from the moment you arrive. This island explodes with colour and superb scenery. Sicily is steeped in history and folklore and it is tied to its past more than any other part of Italy. Here you will see long, interminable religious processions, with madonnas draped in silk and gold, saints smothered in satin and velvet, brilliantly coloured and lit by countless candles, the whole event smoky with incense and perfumed by jasmine. The churches, palaces and customs of the island have a baroque feel about them that is reflected in the food and wine.

Everything you eat in Sicily is luxurious in colour and flavour: marvellous pasta dishes shimmering with silver fish, golden fried fish and vegetables of all kinds; and the beauty of Sicilian cakes, biscuits and desserts is unlike that seen anywhere else in Italy. There is almond flavoured dough which is made into all kinds of brightly coloured shapes, but this is also the home of ice-cream, cooler and creamier than any ever tasted.

Of local specialities, look out for the incredibly complicated Maccheroni con le Sarde, a dish of pasta with a sauce containing pine kernels, fennel, olive oil and chopped sardines; Cuscusu – Arab couscous – which is presented in a version so elaborate that few are the cooks who can make it; and Cannoli, cylindrical pastries filled with candied fruit and ricotta and chocolate. Sicilian dishes will always be completely different from those of the mainland; whatever you eat, the flavour will be strong, the list of ingredients long and unusual and the preparation less than easy.

The island is a paradise for the vine and is deservedly celebrated for its output of generous wines. The most famous of them all is Marsala – a superb dessert wine that can also be served between meals. Corvo di Salaparuta and Corvo di Casteldaccia come in both red and white versions and are consistently good dry wines to drink with good food. The red versions marry particularly well with game. Etna takes its name from the volcano; it is a delightful white wine that has been purified by the lava of the mountain. The noble Faro is the wine of Messina, an aristocratic wine that is drunk for special meals. In addition to Marsala, Sicily also produces a great variety of sweet dessert wines to drink with the pastries and sweetmeats. Sweet Mamertino is the wine that was served to Caesar at the banquet in honour of his third consulship, and there is also a dry version. Malvasia di Lipari is a golden yellow wine with a strong flavour. There are also many muscat wines that vary in flavour from the subtle to the most aromatic.

SARDINIA

This is an ancient land of myths, legends and glorious history, composed of mountains, hills, plateaux and plains. Its rocky coastline is interrupted, here and there, by beaches and small bays. The main activities of the islanders are farming and stockraising, both carried out under conditions of great difficulty. The Sardinians are the proudest and hardest working of all Italians; people who have made their soil work for them against all odds.

Sardinia wants for nothing; there are green fields, woodland, brilliant clean sea, an abundance of flora and fauna from deer to wild horses, cormorants, seals, flamingoes, palm trees and flowers of every kind. Each village and township is steeped in local custom. In Orgosolo, for example, the women traditionally dress in black – even their heads are veiled in black. But in Desuolo they wear red in order to keep to the local custom. These very independent and different individual traditions are reflected in the food.

So different are the ways of preparing food from one village to the next that even the bread comes in completely different versions. Pane Carasau is the wafer-thin 'music paper' bread, but there are many other kinds.

Cheese is produced abundantly on this island. The most important is fiore sardo, a fresh white sour cheese that is used a lot in cooking. It can also be aged and then grated like Parmesan over the pasta which is coloured a violent yellow with the too liberal use of saffron. Then there is pecorino sardo, a little saltier than the fiore, with a stronger flavour. With cow's milk, they make provoletta, small round cheese with a very strong flavour and aroma. The buttery fresa is a round flat cheese with a high fat content, and lastly the creamy dolce sardo, a sweet cheese that is widely exported.

But it isn't cheese that forms the centrepiece of Sardinian cuisine, nor the excellent fish or superb lobsters you will find even in the most humble restaurants, it isn't even the marvellous local game – it is the suckling pig, cooked to this day in the old way, on a spit over an open fire. If it is cooked 'a carragiu' it means that the piglet (or anything else for that matter) has been cooked over an open wood fire. If it's cooked 'a porceddu' it goes in a covered hole between two red hot stones with glowing embers underneath and above. It is always flavoured with myrtle leaves that scent the air. Taccula is feathered game which is cooked like the pig 'a porceddu'. Malloreddus are a very old kind of local pasta, made with cornflour and saffron. Cassola is a marvellous fish stew, highly spiced and very tasty. So many dishes defy translation and must be discovered locally.

The most unusual thing about the Sardinian cuisine is that everything has such an original name and one that sounds very unlike Italian. Even the dish of snails which is the speciality of Cagliari is not called lumache, as it would be in every other part of Italy, here it bears the pompously amusing title of sizigorrus.

Simple cooking this, far less complicated than the cooking of its sister island Sicily, but nevertheless with a great variety of dishes.

The glory of Sardinian wine is Vernaccia, clear, pale yellow soulmate to the incomparable delights of a Sardinian lobster grilled over an open fire. It is also used a great deal in cooking. Then there is Canonau, a red wine to serve with desserts; it has a unique and delicious flavour and is very aromatic. Serve it in small glasses as this is 16% proof! Terralba comes in a red or white version and is a good table wine; dry and smooth, they are of consistently good quality. Torbato Passito is the sweetest of all the dessert wines and has a brilliant gold colour and a marvellous smoothness. My personal favourite is the Mandrolisai which is a pale ruby wine of absolute transparency. It ages well and has a fruity, agreeable and firm flavour.

GLOSSARY

CHEESES

Grana Padano
The northern counterpart to Parmesan, the only difference being that it comes from a different area. This cheese is produced in the Padano region of Lombardy.

Mozzarella
White soft, slightly rubbery cheese that is sold floating in whey to retain its moisture and compact texture.

Parmigiano Reggiano
Parmesan, the cheese most used to grate over pasta or risotto and to add to many other dishes. It comes in huge round wheels which are then cut into crumbly wedges. It can also be bought ready grated and is sold in sachets or tubs. It comes from Emilia-Romagna.

Pecorino Romano
Roman sheep's cheese which is very like Parmesan or Grana to look at, except that it has a black crust on the outside. Very strong and peppery in flavour it is a must for many dishes.

Pecorino Sardo
The Sardinian version of the above, though it tends to be a little more subtle.

Ricotta
Made from the discarded whey of other cheeses like mozzarella or provolone, this delicious, creamy white cheese is used a great deal in the preparation of many sweet and savoury dishes.

DRIED MUSHROOMS

Italian dried mushrooms (funghi secchi) are usually porcini (*Boletus edulis*) and are quite expensive to buy. The consolation is that being very strong in flavour only a small amount is required. They are always soaked in warm water before chopping and adding to the dish. In some Italian shops you can buy very prettily arranged baskets of these mushrooms – they make great presents! But the cheapest way to get hold of them is in small plastic bags which always have a little clear window so you can see in and check quality.

PASTA

The first and most important point to bear in mind when choosing pasta is that there are two very distinct types. The most widely available kind is dry durum wheat pasta which is factory made and comes in an enormous variety of different shapes and sizes (655 at the last count!) from spaghetti to tiny pasta called pastina.

Then there is pasta all'uovo which is made with durum wheat flour and eggs. This comes in packets, factory made and dried, or freshly made and sold soft. You can also make this kind of pasta at home.

To cook dried pasta you must check the packet for cooking time as each make and shape takes a different amount of time to cook. It is considerably cheaper to buy than fresh pasta made with eggs or even dried pasta made with eggs.

Pasta all'uovo cooks very quickly, particularly if fresh. It is generally heavier and more filling than the dry variety made with just flour and water. Most supermarkets sell fresh pasta in their refrigerated cabinets and it is also available from specialist shops around the country.

The average Italian household will eat dried factory made pasta for everyday occasions and save egg pasta for special meals.

RICE

Rice is used in a great many Italian dishes. It is important to use the right quality rice for the right dish.

Risotto Rice is usually arborio and gives the best results as far as making risotto goes. If you use boiling rice to make a risotto you will not get particularly good results.

Riso Giallo is ordinary yellow-coloured boiling rice that is the best variety to use for rice salads or other dishes requiring plain boiled rice.

In soups it is best to use arborio fino, and pudding and short grain rice give the best results for sweets and desserts.

SALUMI

Salumi is the collective term for all preserved meats.

To buy salame, sausages, ham or mortadella in Italy you go to the salumeria.

Guanciale is a kind of Italian bacon much used in cooking but difficult to get hold of abroad.

Mortadella is the largest of all the salumi, an enormous and very heavy pink sausage which when cut produces slices as big as a dinner plate. It is sometimes dotted with pistachio nuts and will always have peppercorns distributed through its length. Very popular with children in sandwiches, it is used mostly in cooking or the preparation of snacks.

Pancetta is another type of bacon used a great deal in Italian cooking and largely unavailable in the UK.

Prosciutto is the Italian word for ham and in Italy this usually comes in two forms – crudo or cotto – raw or cooked. Prosciutto crudo is what you will be served with melon or figs and is used a great deal in cooking. It is preserved, salted ham that has not been cooked. The best comes from San Daniele or Parma. In England it is often called Parma ham, although it may not necessarily come from that city. Prosciutto cotto is the same thing but cooked and is very similar to ordinary English gammon ham. This is also often used in cooking and in the preparation of sandwiches or pies.

Salame is always very dark in colour with whitish spots of fat. This delicious type of sliceable sausage is made all over the country and comes in several different formats. The smallest salame is the stick thin felino and the largest is the huge finocchiona. In between you will find salamino, salame Milano, salame Toscano and many more. If bought whole it must be kept hanging up and eaten quickly once cut. Test salame for quality by squeezing it, there should always be a little 'give' when pressed with the fingers.

TOMATOES AND TOMATO DERIVATIVES

In Italy, two distinct types of tomato are used. The oval shaped plum tomato is used in cooking; it has to be very ripe and red to be cooked. All other kinds of tomatoes, except small ripe round tomatoes, are used for salads. Very large salad tomatoes that are beginning to go soft are sometimes stuffed and baked. Small ripe round tomatoes are used for soups and stocks.

Canned tomatoes are peeled whole or chopped Italian plum tomatoes. In Italian simply known as pelati, they are your most valuable store cupboard stand-by.

Pasta made with tomato in it is an anglicized idea of Italian pasta. I personally would never dream of buying red/pink coloured pasta; the tomato is there for colour and not flavour.

Puréed tomatoes (passata) are available in cartons, cans or bottles. This kind of purée consists of sieved canned tomatoes, free from seeds, ready to pour out and use. A marvellous labour saving product.

Tomato purée comes in a tube or a jar or can and is very concentrated tomato sauce. It can be diluted as required with warm water or stock. Used undiluted it will add body and smoothness to any tomato-based sauce. In Italian it is called concentrato di pomodoro.

TRUFFLES AND TRUFFLE DERIVATIVES

A distant cousin of both the mushroom and the potato this delectable vegetable grows wild in forests underground and requires a dog or specially trained pig to smell it out. Only available fresh when in season they are either black – usually from Norcia in Umbria – or white – from Alba in Piedmont. A very expensive item to buy, but well worth the cost.

Canned Truffles can replace fresh truffles in most recipes which call for them. Expensive, but nearly as good as the fresh variety and useful to keep in the larder in case of need.

Truffle paste comes in a tube or jar and is less expensive than the real thing, yet giving a very passable flavour to any dish.